Also by Tom Cooper:
A@W Volumes 13, 14, 18, 19, 21, 23 & 24

Also by Albert Grandolini:
A@W Volume 19 & 21

Also by Arnaud Delalande:
A@W Volume 19 & 21

Published by
Helion & Company Limited
26 Willow Road, Solihull, West Midlands,
B91 1UE, England
Tel. 0121 705 3393
Fax 0121 711 4075
Email: info@helion.co.uk
Website: www.helion.co.uk
Twitter: @helionbooks
Visit our blog http://blog.helion.co.uk/

Designed and typeset by Kerrin Cocks,
SA Publishing Services
kerrincocks@gmail.com
Cover design by Paul Hewitt,
Battlefield Design
www.battlefield-design.co.uk
Printed by Henry Ling Ltd, Dorchester,
Dorset

Text © Tom Cooper, Albert Grandolini &
Arnaud Delalande, 2016
Monochrome images sourced by the authors
Colour profiles & maps © Tom Cooper, 2016

Cover: A Mirage F.1C interceptor of the
EC.30 – armed with a Matra R.550 Magic
Mk.1 air-to-air missile (wing-tip), and
carrying a Barax ECM-pod (underwing) –
seen while approaching a C-135F tanker
high above the Sahara desert of central
Chad. (Jean-Pierre Gabriel)

ISBN 978-1-910294-54-3

British Library Cataloguing-in-Publication
Data.

A catalogue record for this book is available
from the British Library.

CONTEI

Note

In order to simplify the use of this book, all names, locations and geographic designations are as provided in *The Times World Atlas*, or other traditionally accepted major sources of reference, as of the time of described events. Arabic names are romanised and transcripted rather than transliterated. For example: the definite article al- before words starting with 'sun letters' is given as pronounced instead of simply as al- (which is the usual practice for non-Arabic speakers in most English-language literature and media). For easier understanding of ranks of French Air Force and US Navy officers cited in this book, herewith a table comparing these with ranks in the Royal Air Force (United Kingdom):

Royal Air Force (United Kingdom)	Armée de l'Air (France)	US Navy (United States of America)
Marshal of the RAF	général d'armée aérienne	Fleet Admiral
Air Chief Marshal (ACM)	général de corps aérien	Admiral (Adm)
Air Marshal (AM)	général de division aérienne	Vice Admiral (V-Adm)
Air Vice Marshal (AVM)	général de brigade aérienne	Rear Admiral (Upper Half)
Air Commodore (Air Cdre)	Colonel (Col)	Rear Admiral (Lower Half)
Group Captain (Gp Capt)	Lieutenant-Colonel (Lt Col)	Captain (Capt)
Wing Commander (Wg Cdr)	Commandant (Cdt)	Commander (Cdr)
Squadron Leader (Sqn Ldr)	Commandant d'escadron	Lieutenant Commander (Lt Cdr)
Flight Lieutenant (Flt Lt)	Capitaine (Capt)	Lieutenant (Lt)
Flying Officer (Flg Off/FO)	Lieutenant (Lt)	Lieutenant Junior Grade (Lt JG)
Pilot Officer (Plt Off/PO)	Sous-Lieutenant (S-Lt)	Ensign (Ens)
Chief Warrant Officer (WO)	Aspirant (Asp) /Major[1]	Master Chief Petty Officer

GLOSSARY

4WD	Four-wheel drive
AAM	air-to-air missile
AB	Air Base
AdA	Armée de l'Air (French Air Force)
AdT	Armée de Terre (French Army)
AEW	Airborne early warning
AFB	Air Force Base (used for US Air Force bases)
AMI	Aeronautica Militare Italiana (Italian Air Force)
AML	Automitrailleuse Légère (class of wheeled armoured cars manufactured by Panhard)
APC	Armoured Personnel Carrier
ATAF	Allied Tactical Air Force
ATGM	anti-tank guided missile
AWACS	Airborne Early Warning & Control System
B/N	bombardier/navigator (US Navy)
C2	command & control
CAP	Combat Air Patrol
CAS	Close Air Support
CBU	cluster bomb unit
CDR	Conseil Démocratique Révolutionaire (Democratic Revolutionary Council)
CFB	Canadian Forces Base
CIA	Central Intelligence Agency (USA)
c/n	construction number
CO	Commanding Officer
CSAR	Combat Search and Rescue
CV	Carrier, Vertical (hull classification for US Navy's aircraft carriers)
CVBG	Carrier Battle Group
CVN	Carrier, Vertical, Nuclear (hull classification for US Navy's nuclear-powered aircraft carriers)
CVW	Carrier, Vertical, Wing (composite carrier air wings embarked onboard USN carriers)
CW	Chemical weapons
DGSE	Direction Générale de la Sécurité Extérieure (Directorate-General for External Security; French external intelligence agency operating under the direction of the French ministry of Defence)
ECM	Electronic countermeasures
ECS	Electronic Combat Squadron (USAF)
ECW	Electronic Combat Wing (USAF)
ELINT	Electronic intelligence
FAC	Forward air controllers
FANT	Forces Armées Nationales du Tchad (National Army of Chad)
FAP	Forces Armées Poulaires
FIR	Flight Information Region
FLIR	Forward-looking infra-red
GCHQ	General Communication Headquarters (British counterpart to the NSA)
GCI	Ground-controlled Interception
GUNT	Gouvernement d'Union Nationale de Transition (Transitional National Government of Chad)
HARM	High-speed anti-radar
HQ	headquarters
HUMINT	human intelligence
IADS	integrated air defence system
IAP	International Airport
IFF	Identification Friend or Foe
IFR	in-flight refuelling
IFV	Infantry fighting vehicle
Il	Ilyushin (the design bureau led by Sergey Vladimirovich Ilyushin, also known as OKB-39)
IrAF	Iraqi Air Force
IRIAF	Islamic Republic of Iran Air Force
IRGC	Islamic Revolutionary Guard Corps
KDS	Komitet za Darzhavna Signurnost (State Security of Bulgaria)
KIA	killed in action
Km	kilometre
LAAF	Libyan Arab Air Force
LORAN	radio navigation system
LSK	Luftstreitkräfte (Air Force of former East Germany)

LTV	Ling-Temco-Vought
MANPADS	man-portable air defence system(s) – light surface-to-air missile system that can be carried and deployed in combat by a single soldier
MBT	Main Battle Tank
Mi	Mil (Soviet/Russian helicopter designer and manufacturer)
MiG	Mikoyan i Gurevich (the design bureau led by Artyom Ivanovich Mikoyan and Mikhail Iosifovich Gurevich, also known as OKB-155 or MMZ 'Zenit')
MPA	maritime patrol aircraft
MPI	Mathematisch-Physikalischer Institut (Military Intelligence of former East Germany)
MRCA	Multi-Role Combat Aircraft
MRLS	Multiple rocket launcher systems
NATO	North Atlantic Treaty Organization
Nav/attack	Used for navigation and to aim weapons against surface target
NBC	nuclear, biological, chemical
NCO	Non-commissioned officer
NSA	National Security Agency (USA)
NVG	night vision goggles
OTRAG	Orbital Transport und Raketen AG
PLO	Palestinian Liberation Organization
RAMa	Régiment d'Artillerie de Marine (Marine Artillery Regiment)
RAP	Régiment d'Artillerie Aéroportée (Airborne Artillery Regiment)
REI	Régiment Etranger d'Infanterie (Infantry Regiment of the Foreign Legion)
RHAW	Radar homing and warning system
RIMa	Régiment d'Infanterie de Marine (Marine Infantry Regiment)
RIO	Radar Intercept Officer (USN)
RoE	Rules of Engagement
RPG	Rocket Propelled Grenade
SA-2 Guideline	ASCC codename for S-75 Dvina, Soviet SAM system
SAM	surface-to-air missile
SAR	Search and rescue
SEAD	suppression of enemy air defences
SEPECAT	Société Européenne de Production de l'Avion d'École de Combat et d'Appui Tactique (European Company for the Production of a Combat Trainer and Tactical Support Aircraft)
SIGINT	signals intelligence
Su	Sukhoi (the design bureau led by Pavel Ossipowich Sukhoi, also known as OKB-51)
SyAAF	Syrian Arab Air Force
Technical	improvised fighting vehicle (typically an open-backed civilian 4WD modified to a gun truck)
TEL	transporter-erector-launcher
TFR	terrain following radar
TFS	Tactical Fighter Squadron
TFW	Tactical Fighter Wing
TOT	time-on-target
TPS	Tactical Paint Scheme (USN)
TRAM	Target Recognition and Attack Multisensor
TWA	Trans World Airlines
UAV	Unmanned aerial vehicle
US$	United States Dollar
USAF	United States Air Force
USAFE	USAF Europe
USN	United States Navy
USS	United States Ship (prefix for US Navy's commissioned ships while in active commission)
USSR	Union of Soviet Socialist Republics (or Soviet Union)
WSO	Weapons System Officer (USAF)
ZSU	Zenitnaya Samokhodnaya Ustanovka (self-propelled anti-aircraft artillery)

ADDENDA/ERRATA:

LIBYAN AIR WARS PARTS 1 AND 2

Researching recent military history – especially in the case of such complex conflicts as those involving Libya in the 1970s and 1980s – is a never-ending task. It often happens that important information either arrives much too late for publishing in a specific volume, or must be omitted for reasons of space. In other cases, new or more detailed information appears from new sources precisely in reaction to a specific publication. The authors would therefore like to make the following amendments and corrections to two earlier volumes.

Part 1, Chapter 2: Million-Man Army, p. 25

Several readers have requested additional information about the Sukhoi Su-22M-2K variant cited in Part 1 of this mini-series. Namely, none of the usually available Russian-language publications mentions any such variant; and not only that: no such aircraft were ever manufactured in the former Union of Soviet Socialist Republics (USSR, Soviet Union), and this designation is entirely unknown in the public elsewhere. Nevertheless, according to several Iraqi, one Libyan, and numerous Syrian sources, the Su-22M-2K variant not only existed: indeed, it is still operational with the Syrian Arab Air Force (SyAAF).

An explanation for this controversy was provided by Brigadier-General Ahmad Sadik during the work on the book *Iraqi Fighters* (see Bibliography). According to Sadik, the designation Su-22M-

2K was used for the first time in 1981, for six Su-22Ms from No. 5 Squadron Iraqi Air Force (IrAF) that the Soviets agreed to upgrade (in Iraq) with the introduction of avionics and the addition of the ventral fin used on the Su-22M-3K.[2] Equipment-wise, the major difference between the Su-22M and Su-22M-2K was that the latter was compatible with the Myetel targeting pod necessary for deployment of Soviet-made Kh-28C and Kh-28E anti-radar missiles (ASCC-code AS-9 Kyle; licence-manufactured in Iraq as Nissan-28). Once this conversion proved a success, Iraqis ordered additional equipment necessary for conversion of further aircraft, and by 1988 all of their surviving Su-22Ms – about 30 aircraft in total – were converted to the Su-22M-2K standard.

Similarly, Syria acquired 40 Su-22M in 1979–1982 (serials in range 2500-2599) and 20 Su-22M-3Ks in 1983 (serials in range 3000-3019). Nevertheless, all of their Su-22M-pilots called their aircraft Su-22M-2K, and all available photographs and videos of Syrian Su-22Ms with serials in the above-mentioned range show Su-22M-3K-like aircraft. This means that the SyAAF (Syrian Arab Air Force) put its Su-22Ms through a similar conversion as the IrAF did, at an unknown date in the 1980s.

As mentioned in Part 1, it remains unclear whether Libyans put their Su-22Ms through a similar upgrade. Available photographs distinctly show a number of Su-22Ms that were still in service with No. 1032 Squadron in the 2008–2010 period for example, together with a number of aircraft that look like Su-22M-3Ks. Nevertheless, at least one former Libyan pilot interviewed in the course of research for this project did mention the Su-22M-2K variant as in service with the Libyan Arab Air Force (LAAF) during the 1980s. This might mean that it is at least possible that what appear to have been Su-22M-3Ks, were actually Su-22M-2Ks – i.e. former Su-22M brought to Su-22M-3K-standard.

A LAAF Su-22M in 2009, following an overhaul in Russia. Lack of a ventral fin indicates that this aircraft was not upgraded to Su-22M-2-standard. (Photo by Chris Lofting)

Another of the LAAF Sukhois photographed at the same time was this example, for which it is unclear if it was one of the survivors from a batch of Su-22M-3Ks delivered to Libya in the late 1970s and early 1980s, or if it was one of the few Su-22Ms upgraded to Su-22M-2K standard. (Photo by Chris Lofting)

Part 1, Chapter 3: Chadian Prequel, p. 31

Searching further through his collection, Albert Grandolini found these two photographs that illustrate the installation of 20mm cannons on a French Air Force (Armée de l'Air, AdA) Nord Aviation N.2501D Noratlas transport. One such 'gunship' (serial 15) was operated by AdA in Chad, in 1969 and 1970.

A view from the rear towards the front, showing the barrel of the 20mm cannon on the Noratlas serial number 15. (Albert Grandolini Collection)

A detailed view of the 20mm cannon and its installation in the side doors of the Noratlas serial number 15. (Albert Grandolini Collection)

Part 1, Chapter 6: Showdown in Chad, p. 57

With the help of a reader who prefers to remain anonymous, the authors were able to find additional details about the worst French military loss in the course of Operation Manta, run in Chad from August 1983 until September 1984. Nine soldiers of the 17e Régiment du Genie Parachutiste of the French Army (Armée de Terre, AdT) were killed on 7 April 1984. The troops in question belonged to a patrol sent to inspect a reportedly 'abandoned Libyan T-72 main battle tank' (MBT). Obviously, a T-72 MBT was a very attractive 'war prize' of the time, and it is not surprising the French military decided to find out if the vehicle in question was indeed a T-72 and, if possible, to recover it. There are at least three versions about what happened to them. According to one, the abandoned MBT was 'surrounded by mines', and one of these was tripped by the French on their arrival. According to another version, an explosive charge was inside the tank and was activated by the French when they climbed on the tank or attempted to enter it. According to the third version, one of the French troops accidentally dropped a shell while moving it, causing a massive conflagration that killed him and eight of his comrades.

Part 2, Chapter 1: Libyan Air Force in Early 1980s, p. 19

Comments by one of the interviewed Libyan MiG-23-pilots stipulating that the LAAF replaced the Soviet-made R-23 air-to-air missiles of its MiG-23MFs, with R-24 missiles delivered together with MiG-23MLs, prompted several readers to contact us with related corrections and questions. Generally available publications about MiG-23s stress that not even the early sub-variants of the MiG-23ML were compatible with the R-24, and that this combination only became possible when the Saphir 23MLA radar system was introduced into service – with later sub-variants. Therefore, deployment of R-24 from earlier variants like the MiG-23MF should have been impossible.

However, further investigation in this regards has revealed that the issue was not really that of radars and MiG-23-variants, but of fine-tuning the weapons system and using modified launch rails required by R-24s. The R-24 could be deployed from earlier sub-variants of the MiG-23ML and even from MiG-23MFs, but the problem was that their MVA-23 weapons system would consider them to be R-23s. This issue could be solved if the necessary parameters of the R-24 were programmed into the AVM-23, enabling it to fully exploit the capabilities of the new weapon. Furthermore, the deployment of the R-24 required the use of APU-23M1E launch rails instead of older APU-23Ms.

The question of why the Libyans began utilizing R-24s instead of R-23s was partially answered on p. 19 of Part 2: because they were disappointed with the earlier weapon. The other part of the answer lies in Libyan-Soviet relations. After repeated defeats in clashes with the United States Navy (USN), Tripoli pressed Moscow very hard for delivery of more advanced aircraft, including such types as the MiG-29. Unlike earlier – when the Soviets could afford to ignore requests from their export customers, or outright 'dump' specific types upon some of them – times had changed by the mid-1980s. Due to its precarious economic situation, Moscow began welcoming opportunities to earn hard currency through exporting arms, and thus became more responsive to demands from such 'paying customers' as Libya. However, as of 1985, the USSR still could not export any MiG-29s: their series production began only two years earlier, and was still ramping up, while there was a massive demand from Soviet air force units facing NATO

in Central Europe during the Cold War. Therefore, Moscow offered more advanced MiG-23MLs as an alternative, and a batch of these was manufactured and delivered to Libya as soon as the production run for between 50 and 55 MiG-23MLs for Iraq was complete in 1985.

Overall, the conclusion is that the LAAF began replacing R-23s with R-24s on its MiG-23MFs and MiG-23MLs due to a combination of factors, such as Libyan disappointment with the R-23 and Russian inability to deliver more advanced interceptors. The LAAF was thus left with no option but to adapt more advanced armament to older, less-capable variants of its MiGs.

Part 2, Chapter 4: Operation Épervier, p. 41

Several former LAAF pilots interviewed in the course of research for this project have mentioned a claim by one of their colleagues flying MiG-23s to have shot down a 'French Mirage' over Chad – either 'sometime in 1986' or, more precisely, 'in February 1986'. The authors have attempted to find evidence for such a claim for years, without success: according to all available French sources – official or unofficial – the AdA never engaged any Libyan aircraft in air combat over Chad, nor suffered any losses to them.

However, in his book 'Sabre au clair et pied au plancher: mémoires', French investigative journalist Gérard de Villiers makes an exception to this rule. According to de Villiers, the loss in question happened in the course of what is usually known as the 'FANT counter-attack on Oued Fama and Oum Chalouba', better known as one of most influential battles of early 1986; indeed, one that prematurely sealed the fate of the fourth Libyan military intervention in Chad. This counter-attack was actually spear-headed by a group of mercenaries recruited by the French General Directorate for External Security (Direction Générale de la Sécurité Extérieure, DGSE). Armed with weapons the DGSE purchased from Poland and applying 'useless' tactics, the 'brave' mercenaries should have taken Oum Chalouba in the course of a battle that raged on 13 and 14 February 1986, despite 'suffering some losses'. Without going into any further details, de Villiers concluded his report with, 'they fought for France, whatever they were. A tribute to them should be made here – also for a French pilot shot down by Libyans, whose loss was discretely covered up'.[3]

While never citing any kind of losses over Chad during this period, official French sources confirm that this Chadian ground operation was supported by a reconnaissance sortie of SEPECAT Jaguar As of the French Air Force, on 12 February 1986. These did not suffer any losses. Another mission was undertaken by Dassault Mirage IV reconnaissance bombers within the frame of Operation Scienne: although records about this operation remain cloaked in secrecy, it resulted in no losses. Therefore, it seems that if any 'French' aircraft was shot down, the type in question was most likely some light aircraft operated on behalf of the DGSE-run mercenary outfit.

Should de Villiers' report ever be confirmed, it would represent a confirmation for the sole air-to-air victory ever scored by the Libyan Arab Air Force.

Part 2, Chapter 1: Libyan Air Force in Early 1980s, pp. 12–14; Chapter 4: Operation Épervier, pp. 44–45

There seems to be no end of discussions related to the supposed involvement of East German military and/or intelligence services in Libyan combat operations in Chad. Corresponding reports began surfacing in the media in 1987, when several West European dailies claimed that East Germans were flying Tupolev Tu-22 bombers of the LAAF. Similar statements were repeated by a number of French veterans who used to serve in Chad in the 1980s, and then in some of the specialized English-language press from the 1990s onwards.[4] They were following hard on the heels of reports about the supposed presence of East German advisors, and even some pilots, on the side of the Egyptian Air Force and Iraqi Air Force during earlier conflicts with Israel and Iran.

Despite insistence by several French, Italian and at least one well-positioned US source that East Germans had at least supported LAAF Tu-22 operations through helping in their planning, after years of related research – lately supported by German historian Thomas Müller – the authors are forced to conclude that there is no firm evidence for such involvement. Neither the official records of the former East German Air Force (Luftstreitkräfte, LSK) nor of the former Mathematical-Physical Institute (Mathematisch-Physikalischer Institut, MPI – code name for the former East German Military Intelligence) provide any evidence about some kind of East German military involvement in Libya. Furthermore, the LSK never operated any bomber aircraft (except for a few Ilyushin Il-28s used for target-towing purposes), and thus needed no experience even in planning their operations, as some sources have stressed time and again.

There is no doubt that the MPI had its officers – so-called 'Legalisten' (Legalists) attached to nearly every East German embassy in the Middle East and Africa, and that they were responsible for collecting intelligence from local sources. Although one of them was quite successful in finding out the date of the Egyptian-Syrian attack on the Israeli-occupied Sinai and Golan Heights on 6 October 1973 – several days in advance – generally, the intelligence they were collecting was considered as 'of little value' in Berlin.[5] Moreover, available documentation is quite clear that – always concerned about possible negative repercussions – the East German government was strictly against any kind of military involvement abroad that could result in direct involvement of its military personnel in combat operations. For such and similar reasons, it never granted permission for its military to become involved in combat, even when some of its units were present in conflict zones such as Syria in 1973 or Mozambique in 1981.[6]

What might have prompted reports about East German-pilots in the LAAF's Tu-22 operations remains unclear. However, it is possible that they are related to the presence of light-haired Czechoslovak instructors who served with the LAAF's No. 1039 Squadron while this was deployed in northern Chad (see Part 2 for details).

An alternative version of such reports cites the involvement

This SEPECAT Jaguar A – serial A137, coded 11-RO – was Carbon's mount during the raid on Wadi Doum AB on 16 January 1986. (André Carbon Collection)

This photograph shows the underside of the same Jaguar, together with the centreline hardpoint on which 12 BAP-100 runway-cratering bombs were loaded for the attack on Wadi Doum AB. (André Carbon Collection)

Commandant Carbon cheers on his return to N'Djamena IAP (International Airport), after the successful strike of 16 January 1986. (André Carbon Collection)

Splinter damage on one of the last pair of Jaguars that attacked Wadi Doum AB on 16 January 1987. The aircraft received a hit from shrapnel or debris thrown up by SAMP-250 bombs dropped by the Leader and Number 2 of the same formation. (André Carbon Collection)

of Bulgarian pilots in LAAF operations over Chad. Closer investigation of the activity of Bulgarians in Libya has shown that while few of their advisors served with the Libyan military, most of them worked in the health system and various other public-related projects. The only Bulgarian 'military' service that became seriously involved in Libya was the little-known military intelligence agency KDS. This is known to have cooperated with various Libyan security agencies through a network of local contacts and in close cooperation with the Soviet KGB. This cooperation was most effective in the timely thwarting of several internal mutinies. In early 1986, it was less effective when trying to warn Gaddafi about impending clashes with the USA. With the help of intelligence collected from well-positioned sources in Great Britain, Greece and France, Bulgarians found out that the White House requested over-flight rights from France and Spain. A team of military intelligence officers led by General Todor Boiadjev then prepared a quite precise assessment about what targets in Libya were about to be attacked by the US Air Force

(USAF) and the US Navy, and correctly assessed that any USAF air strike from bases in Great Britain would require massive support of tanker aircraft. Correspondingly, any concentration of such aircraft on bases like Mildenhall and Fairford would mean that a USAF air strike was imminent. As described further below, while paying attention to some parts of Boiadjev's report, the Libyans ignored the rest – primarily because Gaddafi mistrusted nearly everybody around him.[7]

The overall conclusion is therefore clear: currently there is no evidence about foreign pilots flying LAAF Tu-22 bombers during any combat operations over Chad.

Part 2, Chapter 4: Operation Épervier, pp. 42-44
Commandant André Carbon (AdA, ret.) provided a series of photographs taken during the first raid on Wadi Doum air base (AB), on 16 February 1986. Sadly, these arrived too late for inclusion in Part 2 of this mini-series. The most interesting of them are shown on the opposite page.

CHAPTER 1
GEARING-UP FOR A WAR

The history of military conflicts between inhabitants of the area nowadays within the borders of Libya and Western powers is centuries old. In the case of the United States of America, it dates back to the times of the First and Second Barbary Wars, concluded in 1815-1816. In 1911, the area – then under nominal control of the Ottoman Empire – was invaded by Italy, and saw one of the first applications of air power in the history of warfare. During the Second World War, between 1940 and 1943, Great Britain and Italy – subsequently joined by Germany – fought a series of bitter campaigns for domination over Libya, deploying large contingents of their air forces in the process. Towards the end of this campaign, US air power began appearing in this theatre too. After the end of the Second World War, Libya was administered by the British as a UN trusteeship before being released into independence as a kingdom in 1952. Great Britain and the USA retained two large air bases in the country until 1970 Wheelus Air Force Base (AFB) in Tripoli and RAF el-Adem, south of Tobruq while a small Royal Libyan Air Force was established with US help during the 1960s, but only slowly developed.

The situation experienced a dramatic change following a military coup that brought Muhammad Abu Minyar al-Gaddafi to power in Libya in September 1969. Gaddafi nationalized the oil industry and imposed a number of far-reaching reforms of administrative and constitutional nature domestically. On the international scene, Gaddafi initially pursued the concept of establishing a super-state uniting all Arab countries. While welcomed by some Arab and African statesmen, this idea proved fruitless. Indeed, before long Libya found itself at odds with most of its neighbours, especially

Egypt, which culminated in a short war fought in 1977.

Meanwhile, because of his outspoken animosity towards Israel, Gaddafi also found himself at odds with the USA. Furthermore, in 1973, his government notified the US State Department that the Gulf of Syrte was to be a closed bay and a part of Libya's territorial waters. Stressing that under valid international practice the opening across a closed bay can be no more than 24 miles, while the Gulf of Syrte opening claimed by Libya was over 300 miles across, and that Libya could not demonstrate continuous and open control over the bay despite it being recognized and accepted by other nations, the USA rejected the Libyan claim. Nevertheless, for the following eight years, neither Washington nor any other Western power did anything against this Libyan action.

On 2 December 1979, a mob, apparently inspired by the Iranian seizure of the US embassy in Tehran the previous month, attacked and burned the US embassy in Tripoli. Although Libyan authorities did nothing to stop this assault, no US citizens were killed or injured. The US embassy was permanently closed in May 1980 only after a series of assassinations of Libyan dissidents in Europe and after the USA accused Libya of supporting international terrorism.

Later the same year, LAAF interceptors opened fire at a Boeing EC-135 reconnaissance aircraft over the central Mediterranean, and in May 1981, the White House ordered the Libyan diplomatic mission in Washington to close, suspecting that its personnel were involved in a wide range of illegal (or at least 'undiplomatic') activities, including terrorism. In August 1981, the US Navy ran its first ever 'Freedom of Navigation' exercise in the skies over the Gulf of Syrte, provoking a series of engagements with LAAF interceptors. These culminated on 19 August, when two Libyan Sukhoi Su-22 fighter-bombers opened fire at two Grumman F-14A Tomcat interceptors from the carrier USS *Nimitz* (CVN-68) over the Gulf of Syrte. The Libyans missed, but the US Navy pilots did not: they shot down both Libyan Sukhois.

In reaction to the Gulf of Syrte incident, a number of Libyan hit squads entered the USA with the intention of assassinating President Ronald Reagan. While most of their plots were successfully thwarted by US authorities, in October 1981, Americans felt forced to withdraw their Ambassador to Italy from his post because intelligence services discovered a plot to kidnap or assassinate him. Only a month later, someone fired at the US Ambassador to France, and by 10 December 1981, the situation was considered uncertain enough for the White House to impose a ban on US travel to Libya and request all US citizens to leave the country.

Through 1982 and 1983, the Reagan administration sought ways to confront Libya indirectly, for example through mimicking a military coup in Sudan. This was expected to prompt Gaddafi to deploy combat aircraft of the LAAF over that country, where in turn they would be intercepted and shot down by Egyptian fighters, supported by Boeing E-3A Sentry airborne early warning and control (AWACS) aircraft of the USAF. This plot collapsed when it was revealed by the US media.

Through 1984, but especially in 1985, a series of terrorist attacks targeted US and allied citizens in the Mediterranean. Although the origins of only a few such operations could be tracked back to Libya, Gaddafi proved by far the most vocal supporter of these attacks. When 20 civilians – including five US citizens – were killed by simultaneous terrorist attacks at Rome and Vienna airports, on 27 December 1985, US officials asserted that Libya was involved, and ordered the Pentagon to deploy two carrier battle groups (CVBGs) of the US Navy in a naval exercise – Operation Attain Document I – in the central Mediterranean, in January 1986. Following internationally accepted procedures, Washington notified all interested countries – including Libya – of this exercise, and the LAAF reacted by scrambling interceptors that repeatedly interrupted the US exercise. After a short break, the two CVBGs of the US Navy returned to the central Mediterranean and began operating close to the Gulf of Syrte in Operation Attain Document II, run in February 1986. This time, Libyan and US aircraft had nearly 100 encounters, although neither side opened fire.

USS *Saratoga* (CV-60) and her Carrier Air Wing 17 (CVW-17) played a prominent role during Operations Attain Document I/II/III and Prairie Fire, run off the Libyan coast in January, February and March 1986. (USN)

USS *Coral Sea* (CV-43) – with CVW-14 embarked joined the USS *Saratoga* during operations off Libya in 1986. (USN)

Meanwhile, the situation in Chad – which became another 'hot spot' in relations between Libya and the West during the early 1980s – reached boiling point too. In February 1986, Gaddafi attempted to distract attention from the Mediterranean by launching the fourth Libyan military intervention in this country. Military forces loyal to the internationally recognized Chadian government, along with those from France, responded with a series of blows that stopped this offensive cold. Moreover, Paris launched Operation Épervier on 15 February, which began with an attack of Jaguar A fighter-bombers of the AdA against Wadi Doum – a brand-new, major Libyan air base in northern central Chad. A day later, a contingent of about 600 French Army troops began deploying in the country with the aim of officially bolstering the forces of Chadian president Hissene Habré.

Gaddafi knew that his military was ill-prepared to risk an open confrontation with France. Nevertheless, he ordered the LAAF to hit back. On 17 February, a single Tu-22 bomber flew a spectacular attack on N'Djamena IAP. Although only partially successful – the runway was cratered in one spot and the damage was repaired within two days, while AdA aircraft continued operating from the undamaged part of the airfield – this Libyan action clearly indicated that Gaddafi was not ready to give up his pretentions on Chad. Indeed, after one Dassault Mirage IVA reconnaissance-bomber of the AdA overflew Wadi Doum AB to collect post-strike intelligence on 18 February, the LAAF responded by sending one of its Mikoyan in Gurevich MiG-25Rs to fly post-strike reconnaissance of N'Djamena IAP the following day.

A pair of Jaguars and three Tranall transports of the French Air Force on the apron of Bangui IAP in the Central African Republic, early during Operation Épervier. (Pierre-Alain Antoine Collection)

Firefighters working through the wreckage of La Belle discotheque in Berlin, early on the morning of 6 April 1986.
(Albert Grandolini Collection)

Only a month later, the US Navy reinforced its pressure upon Libya by staging Operation Attain Document III. Deploying three CVBGs into the central Mediterranean, the American began operating aircraft and warships deep within the Gulf of Syrte, openly challenging Libyan territorial claims. Eventually, the LAAF scrambled two MiG-25s that attempted – but failed – to shoot down USN F-14s on 24 March. Immediately afterwards, Libyan air defences opened fire on American aircraft with S-200 Vega (ASCC-code SA-5 Gammon) long range surface-to-air missiles (SAMs). Although none of the Libyan missiles hit, the USN was authorized to retaliate. In the course of Operation Prairie Fire, US naval forces flew 1,546 sorties, 375 of which travelled south of the Libyan-declared 'Line of Death'. They sunk two and damaged at least one fast missile craft of the Libyan Navy, and knocked out the only Libyan SA-5 SAM-site operational at the time. The Libyan military proved hopelessly outmanoeuvred and outgunned, the LAAF was de-facto grounded and the Americans suffered no losses in return.

By April 1986, Libya was isolated on the international stage and under tremendous pressure from two major Western powers. It began to feel the effects of no less than 20 different packages of sanctions imposed by Washington. As well as a travel ban and a ban on a wide variety of economic activities, it was forbidden from exporting crude oil to the USA or importing US oil-production or refining equipment, engaging in trade, contracts, credits, loans and other export-import bank transactions. Nevertheless, Gaddafi continued calling for terrorist attacks on Western powers, especially the USA, and continued providing support to a wide range of terrorist and militant groups around the world, thus directly threatening a host of US and Western national interests.

On 2 April 1986, a bomb exploded on board a Boeing 727-231 airliner Flight 840 (c/n 20845/1066, registration N54340) of Trans World Airlines (TWA) underway over Greece, killing four US citizens – including a young woman and her infant daughter. Only three days later, a bomb placed under a table near the disk jockey's booth of La Belle discotheque in West Berlin killed a Turkish woman and a US Army sergeant, mortally injured a second US Army sergeant (he died from his injuries two months later) and wounded around 230 others, some of whom were left permanently disabled. The next day, a Libyan Tu-22 bomber approached the port of Nice, in southern France, and turned away only after being intercepted by two Dassault Mirage fighters of the AdA.[8]

While the TWA crew managed to safely land their crippled airliner at Athens IAP, averting a much worse catastrophe, before long it was clear that the bombing of La Belle was a 'drop that over-spilled the barrel'. The White House and Pentagon contemplated different variants of retaliatory strikes through much of 1985, especially after the terrorist attacks on Rome and Vienna airports. US and allied intelligence services were actively trying to obtain the 'smoking gun' – firm evidence for Libyan involvement in terrorism. After the bombing of La Belle, such evidence was provided by the General Communication Headquarters (GCHQ) – British counterpart of the US National Security Agency (NSA).

GCHQ intercepted a cable sent from Tripoli to the embassy in East Berlin, announcing a 'joyous event' – a terrorist operation. After this attack, the People's Bureau reported back that the 'operation had succeeded and even mentioned the time of the attack.[9] Now there was no doubt that Washington would retaliate: the question was only when and how.

Selection of Targets and Timing

Following a number of meetings with his closest advisors, President Reagan issued a series of orders for execution of Operation El Dorado Canyon – a strike against a set of carefully selected targets in Tripoli and Benghazi, aiming to deliver maximum possible damage to the Libyan military and terror-supporting infra-structure, while minimizing exposure of US forces to possible casualties and collateral damage.

Although the final order for attack on Libya was issued only on the same day the strike was actually flown, reconnaissance of potential targets in Libya, contingency planning, selection of aircraft types, training of crews and other preparations were going on for months, in the course of which reconnaissance operations with the help of satellites, electronic intelligence and signals intelligence-gathering aircraft (ELINT/SIGINT, respectively), but also with plenty of human intelligence (HUMINT) were undertaken above, around and inside Libya. USAF and USN flying units and aircraft involved in the operation are summarized in Table 1.[10]

Table 1: USAF & USN Reconnaissance Units Involved in Operations off Libya, 1985–1986

Wing	Squadron	Base	Temporary Base
9th SRS (Det. 3)	U-2R, TR-1A	Beale AFB	Akrotiri (Cyprus)
9th SRW (Det. 4)	SR-71A	Beale AFB	Mildenhall (Great Britain)
55th SRW	RC-135V/W	Offut AFB	Hellenikon (920th Support Squadron, Greece)
4950th TW (Det. 1)	C-135C	Andrews AFB	

Targeting selection developed gradually, resulting in a list of 152 different objects. Eventually, the final choice was narrowed down to four, including:

- Murat Sidi Bilal Training Camp in Tripoli, which served as a school for naval commandos and terrorist frogmen.
- The military side of Tripoli IAP, which served as the base for nine Ilyushin Il-76 transports used to support terrorist activity abroad (but also military operations in Chad).
- Jamhuriya Guard Barracks in Benghazi, which served as a terrorist command centre and billeting area for representatives of various terrorist organizations, but also for Gaddafi's personal guards.
- The Bab al-Aziziya complex in Tripoli – 'Gaddafi's compound', his main headquarters and residence.

RC-135Ws of the 55th Strategic Air Wing (SRW) – like this example photographed at RAF Mildenhall – maintained a regular presence off Libya during early 1986, collecting immense amounts of highly valuable intelligence about the activity, equipment and tactics of Libyan air defences. (Marinus Dirk Tabak)

Taken in January 1984, this photograph shows one of the SR-71As (serial 67-7973) that regularly visited RAF Mildenhall around that time: many of their operations saw them passing high above Libya. (Bob Archer)

The presence of a large number of MiG-23s (some of which were operated by Palestinian and Syrian pilots) at Benina AB – no less than 43 of which can be seen on this photograph taken by USAF SR-71s – made this air base an attractive target for the Americans. (USAF)

The reasons for the attacks on Bab al-Aziziya and Jamhuriya Guard Barracks are usually explained as them being intended to have a 'devastating impact' on the Libyan leader, but not a deliberate attempt to assassinate him.[11] The pilot who later flew the leading F-111F into the attack on Bab al-Aziziya was quite clear in this regards:

> No one ever said that our purpose was to kill Gaddafi, but we thought they were telling as much without actually using the words.[12]

A fifth target that was added to the list was Benina AB, a major LAAF air base outside Benghazi, with extensive maintenance and storage facilities for MiG-23 aircraft operated by pilots from Syria, the Palestinian Liberation Organization (PLO) and North Korea. The reason for its selection was the potential threat of Libyan interceptors that could scramble from there to intercept USN aircraft involved in attacks on Jamhuriya Guard Barracks.

Platform Selection

The timing of the attack was quite obvious; mindful of the tragic consequences of the 4 December 1983 daylight attack on Syrian anti-aircraft sites in Lebanon, planners of El Dorado Canyon decided to strike at night. They correctly assumed that the Libyan air defences would be at their lowest readiness rate at that time, and thus unlikely to react in force. A night attack was also likely to decrease collateral damage, because fewer civilians would be on the streets.

An A-6E of the VA-85 Black Falcons preparing for catapult launch from USS *Saratoga* off the Libyan coast in March 1986. By early April of that year, *Saratoga* was already back in the USA, and thus the number of Intruders available for operations against Libya decreased to only 20, with 10 of each embarked on USS *America* and USS *Coral Sea*. (USN)

This decision made the selection of aircraft to be involved relatively easy, because in 1985-1986, the US military only had two types of strikers capable of delivering precision strikes by night and in all weather: the Grumman A-6E Intruder, in service with the USN, and General Dynamics F-111F, in service with the USAF.[13]

More surprising was that the option of using only A-6Es was dropped quite early. The USN usually held at least one, but more often two aircraft carriers deployed with the 6th Fleet in the Mediterranean Sea for most of the 1980s. In April 1986, these were the USS *Coral Sea* (CV-43), embarked with CVW-13, and USS *America* (CV-66), with CVW-1. Each aircraft carrier had only one squadron of 10 Intruders embarked (for details of the composition of CVW-1 and CVW-13, see Table 2).[14]

Table 2: Composition of CVW-1 and CVW-13, April 1986

Aircraft Carrier	Carrier Air Wing & Squadrons	Aircraft Type & Modex	Duration of Deployment & Notes
USS *Coral Sea* (CV-43)	**CVW-13**	(AK)	1 October 1985 19 May 1986
	VFA-131 Wildcats	F/A-18A AK100	
	VFA-132 Privateers	F/A-18A AK200	
	VMFA-314 Black Knights	F/A-18A AK300	
	VMFA-323 Death Rattlers	F/A-18A AK400	
	VA-55 Sea Horses	A-6E & KA-6D AK500	
	VAW-127 Tigertails	E-2C AK600	
	HS-17 Neptune''s Riders	SH-3H AK610	
	VAQ-135 Black Ravens	EA-6B AK620	embarked 9 January 1986

	VQ-2 Batmen Det. unknown	EA-3B AK	embarked January 1986
USS *America* (CV-66)	**CVW-1**	(AB)	10 March 1986 – 10 September 1986
	VF-102 Diamondbacks	F-14A AB100	
	VF-33 Starfighters	F-14A AB200	
	VA-46 Clansmen	A-7E AB300	
	VA-72 Blue Hawks	A-7E AB400	
	VA-34 Blue Blasters	A-6E & KA-6D AB500	
	VAW-123 Screwtops	E-2C AB600	
	HS-11 Dragonslayers	SH-3H AB610	
	VMAQ-2 Playboys	EA-6B AB605	
	VS-32 Maulers	S-3A AB700	

Neither particularly good-looking nor fast, A-6E Intruders were equipped with the powerful Norden APQ-148 multi-mode radar, with excellent capability of detecting not only ships on the sea surface, but also small vehicles and other moving targets against a land background. Radar data was presented to the crew on the Kaiser AVA-1, which was the first display ever to use a cathode ray tube (CRT) showing the basic flight data (such as altitude, speed, navigation information and weapon-delivery cues). The bright display included synthetic terrain/sea and sky, and could incorporate radar pictures and other data for use in all-weather flight, navigation and all forms of weapons delivery. By 1985, all the A-6Es were upgraded through the addition of the Target Recognition and Attack Multisensor (TRAM) turret installed under the nose. This contained a forward-looking infra-red (FLIR) camera and a laser-ranger and marker. The bombardier/navigator (BN) of every A-6E thus became able to acquire the target with the help of the APQ-148 and AVA-1, then switch to the TRAM, using optical zoom to give an enhanced and magnified image, and use the laser to mark the target for laser-homing weapons such as the Paveway series of guided bombs. Alternatively, he could use the laser for detecting a target marked by other laser markers, or for measuring the range for more precise delivery of 'dumb' ammunition. The Intruder thus became one of the most advanced attack aircraft of its time. However, this capability came at the cost of low reliability. Originally designed in the late 1950s and early 1960s, the A-6 proved complex to maintain and its avionics relatively prone to failures. A host of improvements introduced to the A-6E during the early 1980s improved the situation, but this remained far from ideal.

That said, there is little doubt that as of 1986 the USN's Intruders were flown by some of the best-trained naval aviators. After negative experiences over Lebanon in 1983, the USN established the Naval Strike Warfare Center a year later. Based at NAS Fallon, Nevada, the centre began training crews of attack aircraft in the intricacies of conducing sea-based air strikes through provision of highly specialized, advanced tactical air-to-ground training on A-6 Intruders and LTV A-7 Corsair IIs. Henceforth, attack units of each of the USN's carrier air wings that were about to deploy for the usual six-months cruise, were spending four weeks of intensive training in large force employment, suppression of enemy air defences (SEAD), close air support (CAS), combat search and rescue (CSAR) and command and control (C2) at Fallon.

Two additional arguments supporting the 'Intruder only' option also seem to have been dismissed. Nearly all the crews of the two Intruder units deployed in the Mediterranean at the time had been in the theatre since early 1986. They had participated in Operation Attain Document II and III, and several saw combat during Prairie Fire. By April 1986, they had plenty of knowledge about the Libyan military and were much better adapted to local circumstances. Furthermore, they were involved in all processes of planning for coming operations and their tactics were more accustomed to short-duration conflicts of the kind that was to follow. El Dorado Canyon was thus much more 'business as usual' for them than for any USAF crews.

Finally, while arguing over the requirement to hit a number of targets and deliver specific ordnance, political and military planners in Washington went as far as to turn down the idea of redeploying the USS *Enterprise* (CVN-65) CVBG from the Gulf of Oman via the Suez Canal to the Mediterranean – although this would have brought the total of available A-6Es to 30 within less than a week.[15] Instead, Admiral William J. Crowe, the Chairman of the US Joint Chiefs of Staff, explained:

> The carriers could have taken out these targets, but not in one raid (so tactical surprise would have been lost). Secondly, the F-111s were ideally suited (for such a mission). They train over land at night all the time. The carrier training is diffuse because they do a number of things: attack ships, submarines and land targets, etc. We all agreed it was important to present the Libyans with a new axis of attack they didn't necessarily suspect. While they were concentrating on the carriers, we wanted to throw in an element we didn't believe they were ready for or anticipated.[16]

Eventually, the Pentagon decided to add the British-based F-111s of the USAF to the strike instead.

Enter the F-111

The F-111 was created at a time that nearly all aircraft-design teams in the USA were working on true 'monster' fighters: aircraft weighing 40 tons and capable of flying Mach 3. Nevertheless, it emerged in a form of a 'can do all', 'multi-role' aircraft that was supposed to have the speed of a fighter, the war-load of a heavy bomber and range of a transport aircraft. The type was practically impressed upon the USAF and the USN by the US Minister of Defence, Robert McNamara, who insisted that both services adapt one, common type of combat aircraft. Research and development caused many headaches for almost everybody involved. As soon as it could, the USN abandoned its 'custom-tailored' variant, the F-111B, and opted for an entirely new fighter design, which eventually resulted in the F-14A Tomcat. Eager to obtain a 'tactical (strike) fighter' capable of delivering ordnance with pin-point precision at high speed over long-range in all weather and at night, the USAF accepted the design and the F-111A flew its first combat operations over Vietnam in 1968. By then the type had evolved into an aircraft capable of penetrating enemy airspace at low altitude, beneath the radar horizon and thus undetected, while flying at supersonic speed, and still delivering precise strikes against selected targets. This combination of capability to fly too low to be detected by enemy air defences in time, and too fast to be tracked by enemy air defences, was to prove the secret of the F-111's success.

Unofficially nicknamed 'Aardvark' by its crews – because of its long nose and sprawling posture when parked – the F-111 became a large, heavy and complex aircraft, including an internal weapons bay compatible with two 340kg nuclear bombs, but foremost plenty of pylon capacity.[17] Essential outward characteristics of the type were its sheer size, its 'variable geometry' wings and two big, powerful (and very loud) TF-30 turbofan engines. The essence of the type was its speed, especially at very low altitudes. The F-111 could accelerate to more than 1,020km/h (550 knots) while flying only 60 metres (200ft) above the ground.

While this meant that the type was unlikely to be detected while approaching its target before it was too late for enemy air defences to react, and that there was hardly an interceptor in operational service capable of catching the Aardvark, its operational speed and altitude, and the necessity to deliver the bombload with pin-point precision in any weather and by night, required a very complex avionics set. Although the General Electric APQ-113 attack radar took up most of the space in the colossal nose of the aircraft, the actual centrepiece of its avionics system was the Texas Instruments APQ-110 terrain-following radar (TFR). The purpose of the TFR was to continuously calculate nearby obstacles and adjust flight trajectory accordingly: it was designed to safely fly the fast but heavy aircraft very low above the ground or the sea, with no or only minimal aid from the pilot. Because the combination of flying fast and low through rain, haze and by night is extremely hazardous, the APQ-110's computer was automatically subjecting itself to gross performance checks every 0.7 seconds.

While the F-111's TFR-capability was unique in the 1960s, it should be kept in mind that this decade was the last before the invention of microprocessors and thus the resulting avionics outfit of the type was rather bulky and – requiring liquid cooling – heavy. It was excessively expensive too: after astronomic cost overruns and near-cancellation of the entire project, the USAF was forced to accept and introduce into service four major variants of the F-111, all of which differed in regard of their avionics and engine configurations.

As of April 1986, there were two major USAF units equipped with F-111s and deployed in Europe – both at bases in Great Britain. The 20th Tactical Fighter Wing (TFW), based at RAF Upper Heyford, included three squadrons equipped with the F-111E – a variant that retained most of the F-111A's avionics, but had a slightly more powerful version of the Pratt & Whitney TF-30 engines. Although this wing had converted to the type in 1970–1972, its units were initially tasked solely with nuclear strike missions. During the late 1970s, they suffered heavily from a dramatic decrease in spending on spare parts, which not only curbed training but also decreased their mission capability. The situation gradually improved in the early 1980s, but their crews were still busy improving their proficiency in delivery of conventional weapons by 1985–1986.

In 1983, the 20th TFW was reinforced through the addition of a fourth unit: the 42nd Electronic Combat Squadron (ECS), equipped with the Grumman EF-111A Raven – a specialized variant equipped for electronic warfare. Although the operational command of the 42nd ECS was shifted to the 66th Electronic Combat Wing (ECW) at Sembach AB, in West Germany, in 1985, the unit remained at Upper Heyford, and was working hard on developing tactics, training and cooperating with various other Europe-based USAF and allied units.

The situation was slightly different in the case of the 48th TFW based at RAF Lakenheath. In 1969, the three squadrons of this wing converted to the F-111F – the 'ultimate' fighter-bomber variant of the type followed by a fourth squadron, in 1977. It was equipped with the General Electric APQ-144 digital solid state attack radar and powered by a pair of TF-30-P-100 turbofan engines that offered an increase of 35 percent in thrust

in comparison to engines installed on F-111As and F-111Es. Furthermore, all F-111Fs were upgraded in 1981 to receive a most useful add-on in the form of the Ford AVQ-26 Pave Tack system.

While nowadays there is a host of much smaller yet far more capable pods in service with a number of air forces around the world, the AVQ-26 Pave Tack was a true technological marvel of its time, and thus a predecessor of all the similar systems that followed. Installed in a container carried in the weapons bay, the Pave Tack comprised a streamlined tubular 'Base' Unit packed with electronics, digital computer and refrigeration, and a spherical 'Head' Unit able to be rotated at high speed and with great precision to look in any direction below the aircraft. The Head Unit was actually a powered turret housing the AVQ-25 laser-marker and rangefinder with the AAQ-9 forward-looking infra-red (FLIR) camera. The laser and FLIR were boresighted and provided an all-weather magnified clear picture of the target, integrated with the cockpit avionic displays and weapons-aiming system. All sensors were stabilized from vibration and looked through a large window made of zinc sulphide. They enabled the weapons system officer (WSO) to lock-on the laser-marker on the target: the computer would then take over the tracking and laser-marking, keeping the target in the display no matter what evasive manoeuvres the pilot performed. With precision of less than 3m (10ft), the laser was compatible with the Paveway series of laser-homing weapons.

The fashion in which the F-111F delivered its laser-homing bombs was called 'Pave Tack Toss': the aircraft would approach the target at high speed and very low altitude, then initiate a sudden pull-up manoeuvre at a predetermined speed and angle (both of which were depending on the unique ballistics of the bombs carried). The WSO would meanwhile switch on the scope from radar picture to FLIR and start searching for the target. Once the target was detected, he would have to lock-on and activate the laser. The weapons system automatically released the bombs at the necessary altitude and distance from the target. These would then follow a ballistic trajectory until detecting laser energy reflected from the target, upon which they would start to home in, adjusting their trajectory with manoeuvrable control fins.

As soon as the bombs were released, the pilot could turn away and descend to the safety of low altitude. The WSO took care to keep the Pave Tack pointed at the target: if the system lost the

Table 3: Composition of UK-based USAF Units equipped with F-111s, April 1986

Wing	Squadron	Aircraft Type (Tailcode)	Base & Notes
20th TFW	55th TFS	F-111E (UH)	Upper Heyford, blue fintips
"	77th TFS	F-111E (UH)	Upper Heyford, red fintips
"	79th TFS	F-111E (UH)	Upper Heyford, yellow fintips
"	42nd ECS	EF-111A (UH)	Upper Heyford; unit est. 1 July 1983; attached to 20th TFW in February 1984; operational control exercised through the 66th ECW at Sembach AB, West Germany, since 1 July 1985
48th TFW	492nd TFS	F-111F (LN)	Lakenheath; blue fintips
"	493rd TFS	F-111F (LN)	Lakenheath; yellow fintips
"	494th TFS	F-111F (LN)	Lakenheath; red fintips
	495th TFS	F-111 (LN)	Lakenheath; green fintips

Designed and equipped to operate at high speeds and very low altitudes, and deliver its ordnance with pin-point precision in all weathers and by night, the F-111 became one of the biggest and heaviest tactical fighters ever. This is an F-111E of the 20th TFW. (Albert Grandolini Collection)

Three F-111Es and a single EF-111A of the 20th TFW underway over the Norwegian Sea during an exercise in the 1980s. (USAF)

A pair of F-111Fs in the process of taking off from Lakenheath. Notable are the fin-codes and serials applied in white, as was the practice in the early 1980s. (Albert Grandolini Collection)

lock-on, or the laser failed to mark the target for whatever reason (for example because of smoke), the bombs were still likely to hit close to the target because of their ballistic trajectory, but direct hits were highly unlikely. Under ideal circumstances, the Pave Tack turret would remain pointed at the target all the time, and thus give instant post-strike information: the system included a video recorder that taped everything for subsequent analysis.

Operating such precious aircraft, the crews of the 48th TFW had trained on conventional bombing since they were converted to the type. After also experiencing a period characterized by a lack of spares, they gradually reached mission-ready rates of 75-85 percent through 1984 and 1985, and began training formation flying and conventional strikes with laser-homing bombs.

Ghost Riders

The F-111Fs of the 48th TFW were a powerful asset – yet one that had never before been tested in combat. In order to gain additional practical experience in operating the type, the USAF launched a

series of simulated long-range attacks, flown in the most realistic fashion. One of the first of these was Operation Ghost Rider –one of the best illustrations of the extent to which the Americans went in order to properly prepare their airmen for operations against Libya.

On 16 October 1985, the 20th TFW received an order to fly a top secret, long-range mission over the Atlantic and execute a simulated attack on a simulated airfield located in Newfoundland, Canada, south of Canadian Forces Base (CFB) Goose Bay. Ten F-111Es, each armed with eight inert Mk.82 general-purpose (GP) 250kg bombs, and supported by 17 Boeing KC-135 and McDonnell Douglas KC-10A tankers, flew this mission two days later. Fourteen F-111s launched from Upper Heyford at 0425 on 18 October, followed by 17 tanker aircraft from RAF Mildenhall. However, the latter missed the rendezvous point over Machrihanish Island in Scotland due to air traffic delays, ending well behind instead of in front of the F-111Es. Flying on board one of the KC-10As, Dale Thompson nearly terminated the mission:

I finally broke radio silence and told the crews where we were. Finally after about 40 minutes we got all 14 F-111s on their assigned tankers and cycled each one through for a refuelling check of the aircraft systems. Our 10 primary aircraft were all OK at this point, so I sent the four airborne spares home.[18]

During the six-hour transatlantic flight, each fighter bomber was refuelled twice (six tankers provided fuel on the way to the target, and four did so on the return to Upper Heyford). Thompson continued:

When we finally got settled down on track I discovered that we were nine minutes behind schedule and then found that we had an unexpected 75 knot headwind. We increased our airspeed to the KC-10 max. cruise, and finally made up the deficiency by our last checkpoint. The F-111s made their last refuelling and descended to low-level 150 miles east of their first land check point at Bell Island, Newfoundland, where they went into a low-level timing orbit. Each aircraft left the orbit point separated by one minute from the aircraft ahead and flew their night, low-level route as a single ship. The route was flown at 400 feet above the ground and 480 knots on their automatic TFR systems. Total communications-out procedures were followed all the way to the target which was about 350 miles from the coast in point. The terrain in the target area was mountainous, covered by dense forests, and had many lakes and rivers throughout the area: a low level radar navigation nightmare. The target was a simulated runway outlined by five pairs of radar reflectors 250 feet apart and spaced at 2,000 foot intervals. Each aircraft had a distinct aiming point, as we were trying to simulate cutting the runway into segments of less than 2,000 feet. A special support team had erected the reflectors on the day before the flight, and had to rebuild two of them that were torn down by brown bears that night. The team remained on site and observed each aircraft's bombing

An F-111E of the 20th TFW loaded with 12 Mk.82 training bombs (warheads in blue colour) in similar configuration to that used during Operation Ghost Rider. Six Mk.82s installed on the BRU-3A/A multiple-ejector rack were always carried on outboard underwing pylons: inboard underwing pylons were equipped for carriage of nuclear weapons and laser-guided bombs. (USAF)

Taken during one of many training sorties over West Germany in the 1980s, this photograph shows an F-111F of the 48th TFW 'in its element': underway at high speed and low altitude, armed with four GBU-10 LGBs. Note the Pave Tack turret below the fuselage. (Albert Grandolini Collection)

> run, checked our timing, and scored each bomb that dropped. They videotaped each aircraft's bomb run, but unfortunately it was too dark to get good video pictures.

Intensive training more than paid off: the first F-111E was within five seconds of its scheduled time-on-target (TOT), and all eight of its bombs impacted within the simulated runway area for a perfect score. Although most of the other aircraft were up to 15 seconds late and one aircraft failed to drop any bombs on target due to a technical malfunction, over 50 percent of the 80 bombs released during this exercise impacted the simulated runway. After an uneventful flight home, the F-111Es landed at Upper Heyford shortly after 1600 local time on 18 October. The same evening, they ran a throughout debrief of the mission, resulting in an exhaustive after-action report that proved highly valuable for future operations of this kind. Furthermore, a group of NSA operatives who watched and listened to check if their mission had been detected for the next six months was happy to conclude: it had not.

Further exercises of a similar nature followed, and most of them remained unknown to the public. In February 1986, several aircraft from the F-111D-equipped 552nd and 523rd TFS (Tactical Fighter Squadron) of the Cannon AFB-based 27th TFW were ordered to redeploy to Mountain Home AFB, from where they flew a mission against a simulated target at Walton Beach, Florida, accompanied by EF-111As. During March, a number of sorties were flown from Lakenheath to the ranges near Konya, in Turkey, some of which offered crews of the 48th TFW their first opportunity of in-flight refuelling (IFR) from relatively new McDonnell Douglas KC-10A tankers. On 18 March, two F-111Fs and a KC-10A flew across France to the Mediterranean to test communication links between them and the US Navy, while three days later two F-111Fs and an EF-111A, accompanied by a single KC-10A, flew what the CO 48th TFW, Colonel Sam Westbrook, described as,

> a mission to confirm that we understood the Navy's procedure for getting safely through the picket ships when exiting from Libyan airspace to return to the tankers.[19]

The final demonstration was flown by F-111Fs on 2 April 1986, when two aircraft from the 493rd TFS each dropped four GBU-

12s on a weapons range in Germany, scoring direct hits with all weapons.[20]

'Bigger Holes'

While rehearsals such as Operation Ghost Rider proved very successful, the development of the 48th TFW's planning for the raid on Libya was less straightforward than described by Colonel Brotzman. Originally, planners at Lakenheath envisaged the involvement of only four F-111Fs (plus two spares) that would split to hit three targets with GBU-12s or Mk.82 GP-bombs. Their attack would be coordinated with that of A-6Es, and was based on the assumption that not only would Britain issue permission for such a mission to be launched from its soil, but especially that France would grant over-flight permission. The involved aircraft were to approach their targets from different headings within a very short period of time, thus leaving the Libyans only seconds to put their defences on alert and to react. However, Operation El Dorado Canyon was a 'big deal' and there were frequent interventions for changes – from Washington, but from other corners too – often causing severe frustration.

The first major change was prompted by the Commander of the USAF-Europe (USAFE), General Charles Donnelly, who decided to involve six F-111Fs, these to be armed with four GBU-10E/Bs each – instead of lighter and more precise GBU-12s, as proposed by planners of the 48th TFW. Crews of that wing had realized that the GBU-10s tended to land about 45 metres (150ft) short of their target if released from typical Pave Tack Toss from low altitude. This problem was not entirely solved even when data entered into the nav/attack system of the F-111F was modified to aim the bomb past the target to compensate for landing short. The GBU-10E/B available in 1986 was four times as heavy as the GBU-12, while its guidance fins were only twice the size. GBU-10s were thus not only more likely to miss their targets, but also more likely to cause collateral damage. Nevertheless, either Donnelly or – according to another version – 'somebody in Washington' had the final say, explaining the use of GBU-10s with, 'they make bigger holes'![21]

Such decisions were rather strange to the USN aviators involved, as mentioned by Dave 'Hey Joe' Parsons, then serving as radar intercept officer (RIO) with VF-102. He recalled the arrival of three USAF liaison officers responsible for coordination of air force and navy air strikes on board USS *America*:

I ... escorted all three USAF gentlemen who showed up to coordinate the 'jointness' part of the mission. They had beautiful computer-printed routes with doghouses, yet we (Navy) were stunned to learn that their graduates of the USAF's Fighter Weapons School – normally responsible for tactics and weaponry in every squadron – were far removed from [the] squadron while planning routes, weapons etc. In return, they were equally amazed that we had a Lieutenant Junior Grade fresh out of initial training on the A-6E Intruder as a lead planner.

Planning Issues

Another issue with the USAF's part of the operation was that of basing and over-flight rights. All through the spring of 1986, planners of the 48th TFW could never be sure if the British government would grant permission for the USAF to launch a strike against Libya from British soil. It was known that British Prime Minister, Margaret Thatcher, was supportive, but her entire government was not. Furthermore, consulting the British government – which had to be done because under the 1951 Anglo-American Treaty the government in London had the right to veto the use of British bases – was jeopardising the security of the mission.

While the British 'go' was at least likely, French over-flight permission was never certain, although expected by planners of the 48th TFW. Eventually, not only France, but Spain and Italy too, denied the over-flight permission.[22]

To make matters even more complex, the original plan envisaged a raid by only six F-111Fs. By 10 April, this was increased to 18 F-111s – including nine aircraft armed with GBU-10s to hit Bab al-Azziziya, three to strike Murat Sidi Bilal with the same weapons and six to target Tripoli IAP with parachute-retarded Mk.82 bombs. While the planners of the 48th TFW did consider such a sizeable formation, they did so only on condition that Paris would grant over-flight clearance. However, after the French denied the clearance, Washington kept the raid size at 18 aircraft. This fact became known to the 48th TFW only during the afternoon of 10 April – although it added no less than 4,180km (2,600 miles) and up to seven hours of flying time to the mission, in turn significantly increasing tanker requirements and also the probability of equipment failure on one of the involved F-111s.

With only four days left before take-off, the task of finding the necessary tankers and deploying them to the UK on time suddenly become a major affair. Nevertheless, all of the involved USAF officers, flying crews and ground personnel scrambled to do their best and the build-up began on the same day, with the arrival of two KC-135As at RAF

Fairford. These were followed by three KC-135s and four KC-10As on 11 April; two KC-10As and one KC-135E on 12 April; six KC-10As on 13 April; and three KC-10As and two KC-135As on 14 April. Overall, the USAF thus concentrated no less than 24 KC-10As and KC-135s at bases in Britain, in addition to at last six KC-135s already deployed in Europe. By accident, the 20th and 48th TFW were scheduled to run a week-long exercise, Salty Nation, to begin on 14 April. This proved an excellent cover for this massive concentration. A summary of known tanker aircraft deployed to Mildenhall and Fairford during these days is provided in Table 5.[23]

Table 4: USAF Tanker Units deployed to the UK, April 1986

Unit	Aircraft Type	Base	Temporary Base
2nd BW	KC-10A, KC-135A	Barksdale AFB	Mildenhall, Fairford
5th BW	KC-135A	Minot AFB	Mildenhall
7th BW	KC-135A	Carswell AFB	Fairford
9th SRW	KC-135Q	Beale AFB	Mildenhall
19th ARW	KC-135A	Robbins AFB	Fairford
22nd ARW	KC-10A	March AFB	Mildenhall, Fairford
42nd BW	KC-135A	Loring AFB	Fairford
68th ARG	KC-10A	Seymour Johnson AFB	Mildenhall
92nd BW	KC-135A	Fairchild AFB	Mildenhall, Fairford
96th BW	KC-135A	Dyess AFB	Mildenhall
97th BW	KC-135A	Blytheville AFB	Mildenhall, Fairford
116th ARS	KC-135E	Fairchild AFB	Mildenhall
379th BW	KC-135A	Wurtsmith AFB	Mildenhall
380th ARW	KC-135Q	Plattsburgh AFB	Mildenhall, Fairford
410th BW	KC-135A	Sawyer AFB	Mildenhall, Fairford
416th BW	KC-135A	Griffis AFB	Mildenhall
509th BW	KC-135A	Pease AFB	Fairford

The orders received on 10 April forced the planners of the 48th TFW to significantly increase the entire volume of their preparations too. Instead of preparing flight plans and operational briefings for only a small group of highly experienced crews, they now had to do the same for no less than 24 F-111 crews (including

A KC-10A tanker of the 306th Air Refueling Squadron arriving at RAF Mildenhall, in mid-April 1986. (USAF)

18 that would fly the mission, and six spares), five EF-111 crews (including one spare) and nearly 30 tanker crews. Furthermore, contrary to better advice from involved planners, the upper echelons pressed for an attack by at least nine F-111Fs on Bab al-Aziziya, which unnecessarily exposed attacking Aardvarks to Libyan air defences for an extended period of time. Faced with such last-minute changes and dictates that directly threatened the security of involved crews, some of the leading officers of the 48th TFW suffered real heartache. One is said to have threatened to resign: instead of receiving understanding, he was confronted by a superior who told him, in essence, that if he didn't like it, 'they' could quickly find somebody else to do the job.

CHAPTER 2
OPERATION EL DORADO CANYON

Following another briefing and extensive pre-flight checks of all involved aircraft and armament at Lakenheath, Upper Heyford, Mildenhall and Fairford, the very complex process of launching 28 KC-10A and KC-135 tankers, 24 F-111Fs and five EF-111As for the raid on Libya began at 1713 local time on 14 April.

The first to take off were tankers, one of which – a specially modified KC-10A with the call-sign Dobey-81 that served as an airborne command post – carried Colonel Westbrook, commander of the operation. While their take-offs from Fairford and Mildenhall did attract some attention from the international media and curious onlookers, the latter were soon after distracted by reports of a mass-launch of 20 F-111Es from Upper Heyford for Exercise Salty Nation. By the time the first eight F-111Fs took-off from Lakenheath, around 1735, all the camera-teams were already away from the perimeter fences of the US bases. These were fighter-bombers intended to attack Tripoli IAP, which had the longest route to fly. The second wave of 18 F-111Fs started launching from Lakenheath at 1805, followed by five EF-111A from Upper Heyford.

After passing north of London, the aircraft rendezvoused over southern England. To better conceal the actual size of the entire formation from foreign radar systems, they formed very tight formations. Tankers were in the lead, wing-to-wing with each other, and with F-111Fs and EF-111As following closely behind, each flight of four strikers (including one spare) joined their designated tankers. All of this was undertaken in complete radio silence, except for the lead tankers of every flight that took over all communications with ground controllers, even when they were joined by F-111Fs and EF-111As. In turn, the crews of the latter spent most of the next 90 minutes checking and re-checking all systems on their aircraft: when this phase was over, spares replaced two of the primary aircraft that returned to Lakenheath, together with four other spares and the spare EF-111A (for a list of all involved aircraft, known serials and call-signs, see Table 5).

The remaining strike package of 18 fighter-bombers, four electronic warfare aircraft and 21 tankers continued the voyage over the Atlantic in complete radio silence.[24] To eliminate the need for any radio emissions, F-111 crews were advised to approach a tanker whenever they wanted to refuel. Boom operators then coached them into position by flashing small signal lights on the underbelly of the tanker. Once one Aardvaark was topped off, it

A famous photograph showing 'Remit 31' – F-111F 70-2390, the leading aircraft for the attack on Azziziyah compound – during final checks prior to take-off from Lakenheath AB on 14 April 1986. (USAF)

Table 5: USAF Aircraft involved in Strikes against Targets in Tripoli Area, 15 April 1986

Call-sign	Aircraft	FY-Serial Number	Position	Armament	Target & Notes
Puffy Flight					**Tripoli IAP**
Puffy-11	F-111F	71-0893	leader	Mk.82AIR/BSU-49	destroyed 4 Il-76 transports
Puffy-12	F-111F	70-2416	No. 2	Mk.82AIR/BSU-49	aborted after last tanker hook-up
Puffy-13	F-111F	70-2394	No. 3	Mk.82AIR/BSU-49	attack without Pave Tack; bombs fell into an open field (missed)
Puffy-14	F-111F	73-0707	No. 4	Mk.82AIR/BSU-49	spare
Lujac Flight					**Tripoli IAP**
Lujac-21	F-111F	72-1449	spare	Mk.82AIR/BSU-49	spare
Lujac-22	F-111F	71-0888	leader	Mk.82AIR/BSU-49	missed the target, bombs jettisoned over the sea
Lujac-23	F-111F	70-2387	No. 2	Mk.82AIR/BSU-49	missed the target, bombs jettisoned over the sea
Lujac-24	F-111F	70-2405	No. 3	Mk.82AIR/BSU-49	software problem; bombs fell into an orange grove short of target (missed)
Remit Flight					**Bab al-Aziziya Complex**
Remit-31	F-111F	70-2390	leader	GBU-10E/B	bombs fell short of Gaddafi's HQ
Remit-32	F-111F	72-1445	No. 2	GBU-10E/B	misidentified the offset point and aborted
Remit-33	F-111F	74-0178	No. 3	GBU-10E/B	radar altimeter failure; bombs fell short of Gaddafi's HQ
Remit-34	F-111F	70-2382	spare	GBU-10E/B	spare
Elton Flight					**Bab al-Aziziya Complex**
Elton-41	F-111F	74-2403	leader	GBU-10E/B	Pave Tack malfunction; aborted
Elton-42	F-111F	70-2396	spare	GBU-10E/B	spare
Elton-43	F-111F	70-2363	No. 2	GBU-10E/B	afterburner failure and complete electrical failure; aborted; ordnance jettisoned; emergency landing at NAS Rota
Elton-44	F-111F	70-2404	No. 3	GBU-10E/B	missed attack time-slot and aborted
Karma Flight					**Bab al-Aziziya Complex**
Karma-51	F-111F	70-2413	leader	GBU-10E/B	bombs fell into civilian area, damaging French embassy
Karma-52	F-111F	70-2389	No. 2	GBU-10E/B	shot down before weapons release
Karma-53	F-111F	71-0889	No. 3	GBU-10E/B	power generator malfunction; aborted
Karma 54	F-111F	70-2415	spare	GBU-10E/B	spare
Jewel Flight					**Murat Sidi Bilal Camp**
Jewel-61	F-111F	70-2371	leader	GBU-10E/B	bombs fell into an open field (missed)
Jewel-62	F-111F	70-2383	No. 2	GBU-10E/B	bombs hit the kitchen of the camp
Jewel-63	F-111F	74-0177	No. 3	GBU-10E/B	bombs hit the frogman pool and several commando boats inside the camp
Jewel-64	F-111F	70-2386	spare	GBU-10E/B	spare
Harpo Flight					
Harpo-71	EF-111A	67-0041	leader	ALQ-99	EW-support for attack on Tripoli IAP
Harpo-72	EF-111A	unknown	No. 2	ALQ-99	TFR or INS malfunction; provided high-altitude stand-off support instead of low-altitude close-in support
Harpo-73	EF-111A	66-0033	No. 3	ALQ-99	EW-support for attacks on Tripoli
Harpo-74	EF-111A	unknown	No. 4	ALQ-99	EW-support for attacks on Tripoli
Harpo-75	EF-111A	unknown	No. 5	ALQ-99	spare
Debar Flight	KC-10A	17 aircraft			tanker support for F-111Fs & EF-111As from RAF Mildenhall (12) and Fairford (4); Debar 81 acted as airborne command post; call-signs including Debar 51-58 & Debar 81-90
Dobby Flight	KC-135A/E	11 aircraft			tanker support for Debar flight from Mildenhall (7) and Fairford (4); call-signs Dobby 31-36 & Dobby 61-62, 91

Ground crews running final checks on one of the F-111Fs from either the Puffy or Lujac flights (note Mk.82 AIRs installed under the outboard underwing pylon). (USAF)

A close-up photograph of the cockpit of one of the F-111Fs about to commence take-off for the strike on Libya. In the foreground is the seeker head of a GBU-10E/B laser-guided bomb. (USAF)

An F-111F from the Lujac flight in full afterburner during take-off for the attack on Tripoli IAP on 14 April 1986. It was loaded with 12 Mk.82 AIRs and a single ALQ-131 ECM-pod. (USAF)

With its two TF-30P-100 engines at full afterburner, this GBU-10-loaded F-111F is streaking into the late afternoon skies over Lakenheath on 14 April 1986. Each aircraft required four IFR-operations over the Atlantic and the Mediterranean in order to reach their target in Tripoli. (USAF)

would slip to the side and make place for another. Three additional refuelling operations for each of the fighter-bombers and electronic warfare aircraft were repeated off the coasts of Portugal, Algeria and Tunisia. Despite the long flight, all the flying of the F-111Fs and EF-111As was done manually, as the auto-pilots of these types were not precise enough to maintain formation. Simultaneously, each pilot and WSO continuously performed full checks of all systems

to ascertain that their attack and navigational systems, terrain-following radars, self-defence electronic warfare equipment, Pave Tack and other systems remained fully operational. Because of the large size of the formation, some of the F-111F crews were relatively inexperienced. The pilot of Remit-33 recalled:

I had never flown below 400ft (121m) at night, yet our mission was planned for a 200ft (61m) ingress to target. I had never dropped live ordnance. I had never dropped heavyweight ordnance at night. I had never ejected chaff or flares and I had never flown with wartime settings on the ALQ-131 [ECM-pod installed under the rear fuselage of each of the F-111Fs]. I had never refuelled 'comm out' [in radio silence] and I had never refuelled from a KC-10A.

Into the Wind

During the days before the Libya raid, the CVBGs of USS *America* and USS *Coral Sea* paid visits to several ports in the north-western Mediterranean, attracting lots of public, but also all the Libyan attention. It was only on the morning of 14 April that both ships commenced high-speed transits to their scheduled operational areas north of the Tripoli Flight Information Region (FIR). Operating in total radio silence and without any kind of other electronic emissions, the *America* CVBG sailed around the west coast of Sicily before arriving south of Malta, in turn evading several Soviet intelligence-gathering vessels, a *Sovremennyy*-class destroyer, a modified *Kashin*-class destroyer and a pair of Ilyushin Il-38s that were flying out of a temporary base in Libya. The *Coral Sea* and her escorts sprinted through the Straits of Messina before taking position further east and about 290km (180 miles) north of Benghazi. Meanwhile, flight deck crews re-spotted, refuelled and armed all the operational aircraft, readying them for a busy night, while pilots and B/Ns of the A-6Es and crews of other involved aircraft were extensively briefed for their part of the mission.

Libya-related operations began before midnight, nearly an hour before the USAF strike package approached the southern coast of Sicily. As usual, both carriers turned into the wind and then each launched one Grumman E-2C Hawkeye airborne early warning (AEW) aircraft. Mission commander of CVW-1, embarked on board a Hawkeye of the USS *America*-based VAW-123, described his exhilaration upon switching on his AN/AP-125 radar and finding out that the USAF was arriving:

The excitement really started … when we actually started picking up the people on our systems, when we started seeing these guys coming in from the western Mediterranean. … One of the most incredible things I've ever seen is that large number of Air Force aircraft come in. Their timing was incredible – right on the money, within seconds of when they were supposed to be there.[25]

Actually, because of unexpectedly strong head-winds and different operational practices between fighter-bomber and tanker

An E-2C Hawkeye of VAW-123 rolling towards the catapult for launch from USS *America* during operations off Libya in April 1986. Two Hawkeyes from this carrier were the first USN aircraft to get airborne during Operation El Dorado Canyon: one of them was responsible for coordinating operations of the carrier's F-14s and A-7s with those of the USAF F-111s. (Tom Cooper Collection)

With her flight deck packed full of Hornets, Intruders and (next to the 'island') three Hawkeyes, this photograph shows the USS *Coral Sea* about to turn into the wind before starting another cycle of flight operations. (USN)

Another busy scene from the flight deck of the USS *Coral Sea* in April 1986. In the centre is one of two EA-3B Skywarriors from squadron VQ-2 – which served as aircraft for electronic warfare and tankers during Operation El Dorado Canyon. (USN)

The view from the island of the USS *America* at the start of the USN's part of Operation El Dorado Canyon. In the foreground is an F-14A from VF-102 (armed with AIM-7 Sparrows and AIM-9 Sidewinders); an A-7E from VA-46 (armed with four AGM-88s) is about to get launched, with an EA-6B from VMAQ-2 waiting for its turn behind it. In the left upper corner, noses of an F-14A from VF-33 (modex AB201) and an A-7E from VA-72 can be seen. (Albert Grandolini Collection)

crews, the USAF strike package had already fallen more than 10 minutes behind schedule by the time it arrived north of Algeria. To get back on schedule, the entire force then increased speed – causing additional problems to F-111F and EF-111A crews, the aircraft of which became very sensitive to flight-control inputs while flying at speeds of 740km/h (400 knots) or more. The group was still struggling to catch up by the time it reached position north of Tunisia, where fighter-bombers and electronic warfare aircraft were to be refuelled for a fourth time. Because the F-111s were planned to start their gradual descent for attack right after this refuelling – in order to have enough fuel for a high-speed attack and return north or, if they were damaged during the raid, to fly clear of enemy territory – the situation resulted in the first unplanned loss of the mission. The F-111F with call-sign Elton-44 remained hooked-up to its tanker for much too long. Realizing it could not reach the target on time without depleting the safety margin of excess fuel, the crew was left without a choice but to abort the mission.

Meanwhile, at least two pairs of F-14As from VF-33 and VF-102 had joined the formation. Their duty was to secure safe passage of the F-111s as they entered the final phase of the flight to Tripoli. To no little surprise of some of the crews, the Tomcats were soon busy – but with 'disturbances' of a different nature than might have been expected.

Italian Warning

While all the US military personnel involved in Operation El Dorado Canyon – and that was about 10,000 people – did their best to safeguard security of the mission, and not only the final approach of the two USN carrier battle groups but also the huge armada of F-111s and their tankers remained unknown to the Libyans, it was at this point in time – around midnight from 14 to 15 April – that the entire effort was revealed to Tripoli, by one of the United States' European NATO allies: Italy.

As described in Part 2 of this mini-series, US-Italian relations were strained already since the Achille Lauro Affair of October 1985. Indeed, it can be said that they were characterized by deep mutual mistrust for at least another 12 months afterwards. For example, while the Aeronautica Militare Italiana (Italian Air Force, or AMI) increased the number of flights by its Breguet Br.1150 Atlantic maritime patrol aircraft (MPA) over the central Mediterranean during early 1986, these were as much dedicated to tracking Libyan naval activities as to monitoring operations by the US Navy's 6th Fleet.

The situation was similar on the other side and – with hindsight – it can only be concluded that the Americans were right in distrusting the Italians – and especially Prime Minister Benito Craxi. The White House, Pentagon and State Department all preferred not to even announce Operations Attain Document I and II to the Italian authorities. It was only prior to Operation Attain Document II – which escalated into the well-known series of clashes on 24 and 25 March 1986 – that the White House advised Rome to increase defence readiness of its forces deployed on Sicily and 'cooperate more closely' with the US military. In reaction, the Italians only decided to reinforce the air defences of four air bases hosting US military aircraft with Selenia Spada SAM-systems and 40mm Breda 40/L70 anti-aircraft cannons. Former Lockheed F-104 Starfighter pilots of the XI Gruppo from the 4th Stormo later recalled that in March 1986 – during Operations Attain Document III and Prairie Fire – they were scrambled a number of times and received orders to 'fly CAPs in support of American warships' – but never sighted any. Their impression was that the Italian Joint Chiefs of Staff were not aware of what was going on between the Americans and Libyans in the Gulf of Syrte.

At an initial look, it therefore might appear as logical to conclude that the Italians never became involved in Operation El Dorado Canyon in any fashion. Nevertheless, official Italian documentation remains classified to this day. What can be deducted or reconstructed is based on oral history testimonies from several retired Italian military officers, a few politicians and reports from various Italian tribunals related to corruption surrounding arms sales to Libya.

For example, one related report states that two days before Operation El Dorado Canyon was launched, Italian Prime Minister Bettino Craxi warned the Libyan Ambassador to Rome, Abdul-Rahman Shalgam, that Libya must soon expect an aerial offensive by the USA. Craxi's warning was based on the US request for use of Italian airspace for air strikes against Libya. The Italian Premier said that he denied the use of not only Italian airspace, but also Italian territorial waters to any kind of US military forces involved in such operations. Strangely, although certain that the US military would attack Libya, Craxi seems not to have put the Italian military on alert: no dispositions of Italian combat aircraft are known for the period immediately before 14-15 April 1986. Nevertheless, he was to play a much more important role during that night.

As the USAF armada approached western Sicily around midnight from 14 to 15 April, it was detected by early warning radars of the AMI and several F-104Ss were scrambled in response. One of their pilots, Major Giorgio Riolo from IV Stormo, recalled:

The alert bell rang and I took off accompanied by Lt Ruggero Rospo from Sigonella. The GCI [ground controlled interception] vectored us towards a target classified as unknown. While approaching, we activated our radars and attempted several sweeps, but our screens went 'white' almost instantly – due to heavy electronic countermeasures [ECM] deployed by what turned out to be US fighters. We saw them for the first time from a range of about 20 miles. There was a long trail of

Although not taken during Operation El Dorado Canyon, this photograph shows an F-111F in the process of refuelling from a KC-135 tanker – with the latter wearing the camouflage pattern often applied on Stratotankers in the mid-1980s. (USAF)

An F-14A from VF-102 Sidewinders – a squadron that provided two Tomcats as top cover for the USAF strike package against Tripoli. Unexpectedly, one of first tasks of the USN F-14s during the night from 14 to 15 April, was to force away several Italian F-104s that approached 'to inspect' the USAF formation. (USN)

navigation lights – which turned out to be several KC-135s. Before long, we found ourselves underway in the middle of a huge airborne armada, with unknown aircraft all around us. I informed our GCI and decided to leave the area. The few other Starfighters scrambled with similar orders to inspect were aggressively approached by F-14s of the US Navy that asked them to move away – immediately.

The AMI commanders quickly reported the approach of the huge USAF formation up the chain of command, and this report eventually reached Craxi. He immediately made a telephone call to the Maltese Prime Minister, warning him of the US 'bomber formation approaching' the island. In turn, about 30 minutes before US aircraft reached their targets in Libya, the Maltese warned Tripoli of a formation of USAF aircraft over the central Mediterranean. As a result, Gaddafi and his family were rushed out of their residence within the Bab al-Aziziya complex only minutes before bombs began falling.[26]

Libyan Air Defences

Ironically, while saving himself from US bombs, Gaddafi didn't put the Libyan military on alert. Because of this, and despite days of building pressure, the US air strikes caught the LAAF and the Air Defence Command off guard.

Libyan air force and ground-based air defences in April 1986 were covered exhaustively in Parts 1 and 2 of this mini-series, and thus it is sufficient to repeat only that the LAAF was still in the process of a build-up at this time. The primary air defence assets of the air force were four units equipped with about 60 MiG-25PDSs and older MiG-25Ps, roughly half of which were operational at any time. Reportedly, LAAF commanders appreciated French-made equipment much more – or at least it is known that the Libyans always took better care about protection and maintenance of their French-made aircraft than they did their Soviet-made ones. That was especially so with the sole unit equipped with about a dozen Mirage F.1ED interceptors, which appears to have always received special attention and enjoyed privileges. The balance of the LAAF's interceptor force consisted of two units equipped with older MiG-23MSs, one working-up on MiG-23MFs delivered in 1984 and 1985, and one in the process of conversion of brand-new MiG-23MLs, the first of which had arrived in Libya early that year. Fighter-bomber units included three squadrons equipped with about 90 Dassault Mirage 5Ds, 5DEs and 5DRs; one with less than a dozen Mirage F.1ADs; and two with about 30 Su-22 and Su-22Ms. The sole bomber squadron operated about a dozen Tu-22s.

All of these aircraft, units and years of training of their pilots and ground crews were of little value, however. USN operations off the Libyan coast in February and March 1986 had deeply impressed the LAAF, making the US military's superiority abundantly clear. Understanding they were undertrained regarding electronic warfare and likely to be outmanoeuvred and suffer heavy losses in another clash with the USN, the commanders of the Libyan air force reacted to the first of Craxi's warnings by ordering the mass evacuation of their aircraft to bases in the centre and south of the country. One of the results of this decision was that by 15 April, only one out of three MiG-23 squadrons usually based at Benina AB was still there.[27] Similarly, while Italian pilots contracted by Aeritalia continued working up No. 1222 Squadron equipped with G.222 transports, they evacuated all operational aircraft to southern Libya. Only one example was left at Benina AB, because it was undergoing maintenance. It seems that something similar happened with most of the MiG-23s, MiG-25s and Mirages based at Mitiga AB in Tripoli. Nevertheless, the transports based at Tripoli IAP remained in place.

Obviously, ground air defences could not evacuate from the Tripoli or Benghazi area: on the contrary, they now became the first – and only – line of Libyan air defence. As described in Part 2, the LAAF never managed to complete the build-up of an integrated air defence system (IADS). The Air Defence Command thus never separated from the air force to operate as an independent branch of the Libyan military. Nevertheless, as of 1986 it did operate two local air defence systems – 'air defence divisions' in Soviet military vocabulary – with one covering Tripoli and the other Benghazi. The division protecting Tripoli is known to have comprised seven battalions (SAM-sites) equipped with 42 launchers for S-75MKs, 12 battalions with 48 launchers for S-125M1As, three battalions with 16 TELs (48 transporter erector

Warned that a US strike on Libya was imminent, Italian pilots contracted by Aeritalia to train Libyans on the G.222s took care to evacuate most of these aircraft from Benina AB to bases in central and southern Libya. (Albert Grandolini Collection)

A view of Mitiga AB, showing 13 MiG-25P/PDS and MiG-25PU (two-seat conversion trainer) assigned to No. 1035 Squadron, LAAF, in the mid-1980s. (Vaclav Havner)

A row of nine MiG-25PDSs from an unknown LAAF squadron, photographed during one of many temporary deployments at Misurata Air Force Academy AB. (Vaclav Havner)

In 1986, MiG-25s represented the most important interceptor-type in LAAF service. This photograph shows one of the MiG-25Ps based at al-Jufra/Hun AB around this time. (via Pit Weinert)

An A-7E from VA-46 Clansmen armed with an AGM-88A HARM, Mk.20 Rockeye CBU and AIM-9L Sidewinder air-to-air missile, during Operation Attain Document in March 1986. Six aircraft from this unit, each armed with four AGM-88s, provided support for the USAF strike on Tripoli. (Albert Grandolini Collection)

launchers) for Kubs, one regiment equipped with OSA-AK and two battalions with 60 SA-7. These were supported by a number of early-warning radars, including P-12, P-14F, P-15, P-18, P-19, P-35, P-37 and P-40, and height-finding radars, including PRV-11, PRV-13 and PRV-16, all of which were integrated with the help of an information collecting and display system provided by German company Telefunken, supported by an elaborate system of wireless and cable communications.[28] In combination, these systems provided near unlimited radar coverage out to about 350km around Tripoli and Benghazi down to altitudes between 300 and 500 metres above the Mediterranean. Indeed, at ranges out to about 50km, radars deployed around Tripoli and Benghazi were capable of detecting targets down to an altitude between 50 and 100 metres.

First Aborts

Taking no chances in the face of this formidable array of air defences, US planners decided to add additional USN aircraft for protection of the USAF air strike. USS *America* launched six LTV A-7E Corsair IIs armed with AGM-45 Shrike and AGM-88 HARM high-speed anti-radar missiles shortly after midnight, followed by one Grumman EA-6B Prowler (equipped in similar fashion as the EF-111As) and one Douglas EA-3B – an old bomber modified as ELINT/SIGINT gatherer that also provided stand-off electronic warfare support, and alternatively acted as a tanker aircraft. Minutes later, additional aircraft followed in the form of two Grumman KA-6D Intruders and two A-7Es configured to serve as tankers for in-flight refuelling in support of F-14s, A-7Es and the single EA-6B.

Finally, USS *America* launched aircraft that were involved in attacks on targets around Benghazi. These included six A-6Es, two A-7Es armed with anti-radar missiles and three additional EA-6B Prowlers.[29] USS *Coral Sea* launched eight A-6Es and six McDonnell Douglas F/A-18As armed with AGM-88 HARM anti-radar missiles. To the dismay of their crews, two of the A-6Es

from VA-55 aborted early due to malfunctions in their radar homing and warning systems (RHAW) and TRAM-turrets.

Meanwhile, after topping up their tanks for the fourth time, the F-111Fs began descending and forming into their attack groups. In front were six strikers slanted to attack Tripoli IAP, led by Puffy-11. Behind them were eight F-111Fs for Aziziyah led by Remit-31 and three for Murat Sidi Bilal led by Jewel-61, while one of the four EF-111As each joined one of the Aardvark flights. Eighty kilometres (50 miles) from Tripoli, all crews switched off their navigational lights, armed their bombs and performed the final check of their systems.

While descending ever closer to the sea surface, the strike force suffered its next loss: Harpo-72 – one of the EF-111As planned to provide close-in electronic countermeasures for F-111Fs striking Tripoli – suffered an equipment failure. The crew refused to abort and instead took position north of Tripoli, providing valuable electronic warfare support during the attack. Two other EF-111As continued for the western low-altitude jamming orbit off the coast of Tripoli, while the fourth flew further east to cover the F-111Fs that were about to attack Tripoli IAP. Trailing behind the F-111s were four F-14As from VF-33 and VF-102. Initially flying at very low altitude, they climbed and established combat air patrols (CAP) about 40km (25 miles) north of Tripoli. The commander of CVW-1, Commander Jay Johnson, was surprised to realize that the incoming strike took the Libyans completely by surprise:

I came in at low altitude and popped up on the clock and said, 'Holy Cow, this is a city that's asleep!' ... they didn't have a clue.[30]

Because the Italian and Maltese warnings had not yet reached Tripoli, all the lights in the city were still on. Together with Johnson came the six A-7Es of VA-46, that next moved into position to fire AGM-45 Shrike and AGM-88 HARM anti-radar missiles.

Anti-Radar Barrage

Puffy-11 was the first F-111F to enter Libyan airspace and cross the beach west of Tripoli, around 0152. Flying on TFR, the big fighter bomber then continued at a very low altitude over the suburbs west and south of the Libyan capital, followed by five other aircraft of Puffy and Lujac flights. However, contrary to what might be expected, the strike on Tripoli did not start with the F-111Fs dropping their bombs on selected targets. Four minutes before them, at 0156, the early warning units of the Air Defence Command deployed around the Libyan capital began turning on their radars. The crews of VA-46's A-7Es reacted almost immediately, unleashing a devastating barrage of 16 AGM-88s. In a matter of few minutes, the Americans claimed to have knocked out several early warning radars and a number of fire-control radars serving SA-2, SA-3, SA-6, SA-8 and Crotale SAM-sites. The few surviving sites that remained operational were then finished by a volley of eight AGM-45 Shrikes, launched from short range. According to Soviet sources, the heaviest ECM were deployed against Soviet-made P-14F and P-37 early warning radars, while most of the HARMs targeted P-15 and French-made Volex radar working in centimetre range.[31] One of the F-111F-pilots recalled the scene:

As we came up on the coast, I remember thinking, I'm flying the first airplane across the target. We'd had detailed mission planning involving many, many airplanes. But everything was coordinated off the timing of the launch back in England. So if the EF-111s didn't get to their station on time, we were going to be sitting ducks. If the HARM and Shrike ... shooters from the Navy weren't firing their missiles on time, I wasn't sure how many planes we would lose. If the air crews weren't flying the ground track they were supposed to be flying, there was a high probability they would hit each other because our TOT was literally compressed to saturate the Libyan defences. We were completely com-out on our way to the target – no radio communications whatsoever. I had no idea whether the Navy had launched. I had no idea whether anybody was where they were supposed to be.

The first time I ever saw or heard another plane was 40 seconds prior to my bomb release, when I looked up and saw a Navy A-7 firing a Shrike at a radar emitter. And boy, that gave me a warm, fuzzy, good feeling inside.[32]

By that time, the force to strike Aziziya was down to seven aircraft: Elton-41 suffered a Pave Tack malfunction shortly before reaching Tripoli, and had to abort. The remaining three flights approached their target along two slightly different ingress routes to avoid interference by their TFRs: odd-numbered call-signs to the left and even-numbered to the right, with 45 seconds separation between aircraft and a speed of about 965km/h (600 miles per hour). For the crew of Remit-33, the sight in front of them appeared spectacular:

The target run was a spectacle of sound and light. First were Crotales, which skimmed the sea surface emitting a shower of

sparks like cheap bottle rockets. The second was AAA, which included 23mm ZSU 'hoses', 50-60mm 'pom-pom' S2 and intermittent explosions from a large-calibre gun. Finally, either Remit 31 or 32 released a couple of flares that appeared like SAM plumes fixed on our windscreen. Our only reaction was to suck more air.[33]

The crew of Remit-31 flew the first attack on Aziziya, all the time fighting against the TFR that attempted to initiate a '4 g-force' pull-up manoeuvre, probably due to interference from the French-made Crotale SAM search radar that operated on the same frequency. All the time, the pilot had to over-ride the system, briefly disengage the TFR and push the nose back down:

I was worried about the wizzo finding his radar offset point, which would later help him find the main barracks at al-Aziziya. It was absolutely paramount that he find it, so there was obviously a lot of pressure on him. And there were only a few seconds to find the target because we were very low to the ground. He moved the Pave Tack pod to the last few feet of refinement and he had to turn the laser on the target to guide the bombs in. He had his hands full while I was manoeuvring the airplane. It was on auto-pilot – and my hands and feet were completely off the controls – but I had my hand on [the] throttles the whole time to adjust air speed. When the wizzo got squared away, I pulled the nose up.[34]

At a range of 7,000 metres (23,000ft) from the target, Remit-31 entered a gentle climb, the system released four GBU-10E/Bs at the precisely calculated moment, and the pilot then swung the big F-111F into a 135-degree wingover to depart the target area:

In the meantime, the WSO started guiding the four bombs into the target. ... He was saying, 'I've got it. Come on. Impact! Big Time!' Then all hell broke loose. Just as he was guiding the bombs into the target, a ZSU opened up. It's an AAA-gun, 23mm, four barrels, very effective. I could see the tracers coming up at us from about our seven o'clock position. The WSO said our bombs made impact so I descended to low level to get back over the water. It was then that I made my one and only radio call on the raid, 'Feet Wet', meaning we were over the sea, and 'Tranquil Tiger', meaning a successful attack.[35]

Remit-32 missed the offset point but the crew realized the error and cancelled their bomb run. The F-111F headed out to sea to jettison their ordnance, closely pursued by at least three SA-8s, one of them passing close enough for the pilots to see its fins and exhaust. His radio report was not as positive as that of the formation leader, ending with 'frosty freezer' – which meant an abort.

Remit-33 overcame the same TFR problem as its flight lead, disengaged the afterburner and reset the wings to a 54-degrees sweep while ejecting chaff and flares. Approaching to 7,000 metres from the target, the pilot initiated the Pave Tack Toss manoeuvre,

An EF-111A of the 42nd ECS: four of these highly-sophisticated aircraft for electronic warfare provided stand-off jamming for F-111Fs that attacked Tripoli. Combined with AGM-88 HARMs fired by USN's A-7Es, electronic countermeasures emitted by them proved highly effective in suppressing most of Libyan air defences. (Albert Grandolini Collection)

Although not taken during El Dorado Canyon, this photograph nicely illustrates the configuration of nine F-111Fs which attacked Bab al-Aziziya compound in Tripoli: wings swept back, armed with four GBU-10E/Bs and with the Pave Tack pod rotated down to enable its sensor 'head' to acquire and mark targets. (USAF)

The front side of Gaddafi's residence inside the Bab al-Aziziya compound, shattered by near-misses from a total of eight GBU-10s released by Remit-31 and Remit-33. (Albert Grandolini Collection)

and bombs were released. However, as the pilot entered a 110-degree left bank, the WSO could not hold the target on his FLIR scope: surface winds that had shifted from their predicted direction, smoke and debris thrown up by Remit-31's bombs obscured the target, and bombs thus went ballistic, impacting the ground short of a large administration building within the Aziziya compound. Remit-33 was chased away by an SA-8, the pilot sweeping the wings back to 72 degrees and accelerating to 1,222km/h (660 knots).[36]

None of the eight bombs released by Remit-31 and Remit-33 scored a direct hit: detonating in two lines between Gaddafi's ceremonial tent, his residence and an administration building, they shattered all windows and doors, collapsed a few walls and caved-in the roofs of nearby buildings. An aviator from USS

America recalled the sight and the chaotic reaction of the Libyan SAM-sites that fired several missiles without any radar guidance:

> Their bombs looked to me like they were right on target. It appeared to me that if there was collateral damage in Tripoli, it was done by Libyans themselves firing missiles straight up into the air and which then came down on the city.[37]

The crew to experience the biggest problems during the attack on Aziziya was that of Elton-43. Completely on its own after two other F-111Fs from this flight aborted, it then experienced a series of technical malfunctions. The crew first ignored the Master Caution light that indicated that very hot air was probably leaking into the main landing gear well, threatening to explode the tyres and adjacent fuel tanks. But then a complete electrical failure ended their mission: left without all avionics and instrumentation, the crew was left with no choice but to head north, using a hand torch to see their standby compass.

Loss of Karma-52

The fifth F-111F to reach the target area became only the third aircraft to release its weapons: ignoring the failure of their TFR-system, the crew of Karma-51 pressed on and entered the Pave Tack Toss at 7,000 metres from the target. However, after his bombs separated, the WSO could not find the target to guide them: unknown to the crew, they selected the wrong offset point prior to attack and their aircraft was nearly a mile away from where it should have been. Consequently, all four GBU-10E/Bs landed long and late, crashing into a civilian neighbourhood. They heavily damaged the French Embassy, also caused damage to the Austrian, Finnish, Iranian and Swiss embassies, and resulted in about 20 civilian casualties. Ironically, the French Embassy shared a parking lot with the Libyan Intelligence Bureau, and thus the latter was narrowly missed too. Nevertheless, the blast from the 1,000kg heavy bomb killed a senior member of the Abu Nidal group that was inside this building, thus actually scoring the major – yet usually ignored – anti-terror success of this operation.[38]

Although one of the Libyan SAM sites overcame all the electronic interferences emitted by the EF-111As and Karma-51's ALQ-131 jamming pod, and achieved a lock-on, the F-111F came away undamaged.[39] The next F-111 was less lucky: Karma-52 vanished around this time while still approaching its target low over the sea, about 7.2km (4.5 miles) north of Tripoli, under circumstances recalled by the pilot of Remit-31:

> It was a smear across the water. It reminded me of having seen napalm in Vietnam.[40]

Jim Jimenez, the pilot of Karma-53, was thought to have seen Karma-52 crash. Similarly, the pilot of one of the A-7Es that were still in the area recalled:

> I saw an F-111F hit the water at around my nine o'clock position. He was along the attack axis and he may have seen

Captain Fernando Ribas-Dominici earlier during his career in front of an F-111. (Albert Grandolini Collection)

a missile coming at him. At night, whenever a missile is fired, it always looks like it's coming straight at you. So he may have manoeuvred abruptly to try to avoid it and hit the water in the process. I don't know. I just know they hit the water, creating a ball of flame that looked like napalm. And I knew I'd lost some friends.[41]

While nearly all published accounts are uncertain about what exactly happened to the F-111F with serial number 70-2389, it is almost certain that the aircraft was shot down by one of the surviving Libyan SAM sites. The most likely reason is that the ALQ-131 jamming pod suffered a malfunction. The crew of Karma-52, pilot Captain Fernando Ribas-Dominici and the WSO, Captain Paul Lorence, ejected seconds before their F-111F slammed into the sea. Unfortunately, their ejection capsule hit the water very hard before the chutes could fully deploy: they were knocked unconscious and drowned.[42] Jimenez's WSO, Michael Hoyes, recalled that after seeing a flash and fireball just ahead of his aircraft, he concluded it was an F-111 hit by a SAM. Furthermore, he recalled that the USAF was quite quick in correctly concluding that Karma-52 was shot down, instead of hitting the sea surface:

There was a sub off the coast of Tripoli and they reported what they saw regarding the lost F-111 and its two crewmembers. Interestingly, their report was different than that of other pilots: they saw what appeared to be an ejection – which for the F-111 would involve rocket-launching the entire cockpit area away from the jet, instead of ejection seats 'only'. The report from that sub – at least for a while – left us with some hope that the crew might have survived an ejection. Tragically, that ended up not being the case.[43]

Continuing their mission, Jimenez and Hoyes on Karma-53 suffered a Pave Tack malfunction due to a failed generator only seconds before entering the climb. Aborting, they passed low over Aziziya just as the next three F-111Fs commenced their attack runs on Murat Sidi Bilal barracks.

Murat Sidi Bilal and Tripoli IAP
Although the air defences in Tripoli around Murat Sidi Bilal

The highly successful attack of Puffy-11 on Tripoli IAP was immortalized by the dramatic video recorded by its Pave Tack system, stills from which are shown here. The first shows the Pave Tack view of the ramp with five Il-76 transports. The WSO placed the crosshairs at the fin of the centre Il-76 in the front row. (USAF)

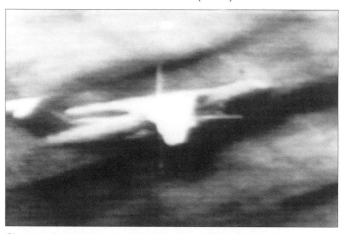

Closer to the target, and only seconds away from bomb-release, the WSO pointed his crosshairs at the rearmost Il-76 in the row, the silhouette of which is now clearly visible. (USAF)

barracks were less dense than over central Tripoli, precise anti-aircraft fire forced the crew of Jewel-61 to descend, disengage the TFR and engage the afterburner to accelerate to a speed of 1,126km/h (700mph) while approaching their target in manual flight at only 24 metres (80ft) altitude. The pilot pulled up at the correct range from the target, but upon release, the WSO could not find the target, and thus could not designate: all four bombs landed in an open field. The crew of Jewel-62 experienced some problems finding their offset point, but the WSO then found the target with Pave Tack and pointed his laser at the kitchen, which was narrowly missed by all four GBU-10E/Bs. Finally, Jewel-63 achieved slightly better results: after bomb-release, the WSO pointed his Pave Tack at the large, covered swimming pool. The dust and smoke from the other bombs then interrupted his guidance system, causing the bombs to fall ballistically, missing by about a dozen metres. Post-strike analysis determined that none of the bombs dropped by the Jewel flight scored a direct hit, but they caused severe damage to the kitchen and mess hall, a classroom building, an administration support building and the swimming pool, and destroyed several small training vessels.[44]

A combination of minor equipment malfunctions and mistakes resulted in similar results for most of the attacks by Puffy and Lujac flights. The sole exception was the first F-111F of this

Swiveling the 'head' rearwards enabled the video recorder of Puffy-11's Pave Tack system to record this image of 12 Mk.82s going off to the left and rear of the targeted Il-76. Although apparently not scoring any direct hits, their explosions instantly destroyed transports registered as 5A-DZZ and 5A-DLL, while the resulting fire heavily damaged three other Il-76s. (USAF)

Many of the supposed 'pieces of American bombs that murdered Libyan civilians' were actually parts of about 30 Libyan SAMs fired at F-111s that were flying low over Tripoli. This photograph shows what was probably the booster section of an SA-3 SAM. (Albert Grandolini Collection)

This Mk.82 AIR failed to detonate and was subsequently shown by the Libyans to representatives of the international media. Notable is the ballute drag device, originally developed for deployment of nuclear weapons from low altitude. (Albert Grandolini Collection)

strike, Puffy-11. The crew found Tripoli IAP well illuminated by terminal lights, aimed for a parking ramp with several Ilyushin Il-76 transports, the pilot made few final corrections in the flight route and the WSO released a volley of 12 Mk.82 bombs. Slowed by their BSU-49 ballute (balloon and parachute) drag devices, most of the bombs fell on the middle transport, immediately destroying it and another parked nearby (registrations 5A-DZZ and 5A-DLL). The resulting conflagration then gutted two additional Il-76s and damaged another.

Fireworks over Benghazi

A-6E Intruders of two US Navy squadrons approached their targets in the Benghazi area in similar fashion to the F-111Fs: in complete radio silence, at the lowest safe altitude and best speed. In front was a formation of six A-6Es from VA-55: one armed with 12 Mk.82 GP-bombs equipped with Mk.12 Snake Eye retarding fins (a combination also known as 'Mk.82SE') and five carrying 12 CBU-59 APAM cluster bomb units (CBUs) each. They were escorted by six HARM-toting F/A-18s from VFA-132, the pilot of one of which recalled about the flight to the target zone:

There was only one radio-transmission as we headed for Benina. We issued an alert as to what missiles would be in the

target area. There had been a lot of pre-strike publicity in the press, and the Navy had had a significant presence in the area for several months prior to the raid, so we were surprised that the Libyan defences weren't more alert. Everything around Benghazi was lit and there was minimal activity.

One of the involved B/Ns confirmed that this attack caught the Libyans completely off guard:

With all the lights on you could see the targets just where they were supposed to be. Apparently, one of the most anticipated surprise attacks in recent history turned out to be a surprise when it was finally started. [45]

The A-6Es entered Libyan airspace well south of Benghazi and then turned north, approaching Benina from a southerly direction. It was only during the final seconds before their attack that the Libyan air defences opened fire, as recalled by another Intruder-pilot:

Once we proceeded inbound to the target, there were a couple of SAMs launched. We were lit up [detected by their radars], so they were looking for us, and they were shooting at us, but as far as I could tell ... [the missiles] weren't guiding.

Trailing behind the A-6Es, an EA-6B from VMAQ-2 and two from VAQ-135 activated their powerful ALQ-99 electronic warfare systems and heavily disturbed the work of Libyan SAM sites. Simultaneously, F/A-18As that approached from the north reacted with four AGM-88s. According to Soviet sources, Libyan early warning radars failed to issue a timely warning about incoming aircraft, despite detecting them 'rather easily'. Supposedly, the radar stations were inappropriately staffed by personnel that were poorly and inconsistently trained. Furthermore, there was a 'lack of direct communication links between early warning radar stations and air defence brigades' [SAM sites].[46] Tasked with providing top cover for attacking Intruders, Robert Stumpf recalled the resulting scene:

A-6 crews … saw the incoming HARMs, orange cones of destruction, smothering SAM sites in their paths. … SAMs that were launched created a sensational effect in the night sky, but none guided effectively.[47]

Undisturbed, the Intruders appeared over Benina AB at exactly 0200 local time and devastated it with precise hits of no less than 60 CBU-59s and 12 Mk.82s. The runway was cratered at several points and at least three, possibly four of the MiG-23MS that stood on alert were destroyed, together with at least two Mil Mi-8 helicopters, one G.222, one Boeing 727 airliner and one SF.260 trainer. An undetermined number of additional aircraft were damaged, together with nearly all of the buildings and one hangar at the base.[48] As the A-6Es raced back towards the safety of airspace over the Mediterranean, Stumpf concluded:

I was surprised by the lack of resistance and found myself with little to do that morning. Nobody got shot down. There was no airborne opposition, no radars illuminating us. It didn't get exciting because we didn't have any opposition.[49]

Further north-west, six A-6Es from VA-34 – supported by six F/A-18As from VFMA-323 and a single EA-6B from VAQ-135 – struck at Jamhuriya Guard Barracks in Benghazi. The main planner of the USN's strike, Dee L. Mewbourne, flew as B/N of the lead aircraft:

As we approached the Libyan coast, the once barely visible horizon took on a surreal image. Underneath a translucent layer of clouds hovering overhead, the city glowed like a candle under a cream coloured veil. … I could discern the patterns of lights defining the buildings, residential areas and roads.

Libyan air defences in Benghazi became active around 0157 local time, firing several SAMs that ascended in white glare towards the opaque cloud layer above the city. One of the USN's aviators recalled the sight:

The SAMs looked like just a little glow trekking through the sky. It kind of looks surreal because how could it be a star going that fast? And then you realize that it might be going for you and that snaps you back to reality.[50]

Once again, heavy jamming and HARMs rendered Libyan SAM-sites inoperational and all of their missiles failed to guide: a number of them fell out of the cloud cover and crashed in Benghazi instead. Two A-7Es from VA-46 then added to the barrage with a total of four AGM-45 Shrikes. Only one SA-6 site fired back quite precisely, as recalled by Mewbourne:

At approximately two minutes from the target, I peered out the right windscreen in time to observe the salvo launch of two missiles. Unlike the previous missiles that changed relative bearing quickly as they passed the aircraft, their glare grew in intensity along the same relative bearing. There was only one

explanation for the difference: these missiles were guiding on us! 'Break right' I called excitedly. Although unaware of the impeding danger, the pilot sensed the urgency in my voice and immediately responded. … The cockpit, normally dimly lit by red instrument lights was suddenly filled with a magnificent white light as the two missiles passed close abeam our airplane. I braced for the warhead detonation … Nothing.[51]

While successful, the SAM break had a very serious consequence for the sensitive avionics of Mewbourne's aircraft, Parsons recalls:

His inertial system failed while they were dodging a SAM still inbound to the target. The B/N resorted to 'Zen bombing', with manual controls, calling 'stand-by, stand-by, pickle!' to this pilot – for a direct hit![52]

Although experiencing great difficulties with identifying their targets on radar in the middle of Benghazi, the crews of all six A-6Es unleashed 12 Mk.82SEs each, with excellent precision. Jamhuriya Barracks were completely demolished. Also hit was a nearby warehouse that served as a MiG-23-assembly facility: four shipping crates containing MiGs were destroyed there, while a fifth was damaged. Two bombs fell wide of the target, hitting a civilian neighbourhood.[53] All Intruders disengaged unmolested: their highly trained crews were familiar with the area, knew the enemy and how to evade.

Table 6: USN Aircraft involved in Strikes on Tripoli & Benghazi, 15 April 1986

Carrier Air Wing & Squadrons	Aircraft	Armament (if deployed) & Notes
CVW-1	(AB)	
VF-102	4x F-14A	CAP
VF-33	4x F-14A	CAP
VA-46	6x A-7E	8x AGM-45, 16x AGM-88 for USAF
VA-72	2x A-7E	4x AGM-45 for USN
VA-34	8x A-6E	2 aborted, attack on Jamhuriya Barracks
	2x KA-6D	tanker support
VAW-123	2x E-2C	AEW
VMAQ-2	2x EA-6B	1x EW support for USAF 1x EW support for USN
HS-11	2x SH-3H	SAR
VQ-2	2x EA-3B	EW & tanker support
CVW-13	(AK)	
VFA-131/132, VMFA-314/323	4x F/A-18A 6x F/A-18A 6x F/A-18A	CAP 10x AGM-88 for Benina raid 10x AGM-88 for Benghazi raid
VA-55	7x A-6E 2x KA-6D	1 aborted, attack on Benina AB tanker support
VAW-127	2x E-2C	AEW
VAQ-135	2x EA-6B	EW support for USN
HS-17	2x SH-3H	SAR
VQ-2	1x EA-3B	EW & tanker support

One of ordnancemen on the USS *Coral Sea* preparing to load Mk.82 SEs on an A-6E of VA-55 that participated in the attack on Benina AB. (USN)

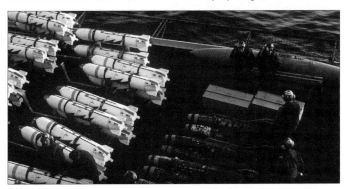

Sailors on board USS *Coral Sea* stacking Mk.59 APAM CBUs (white containers) and Mk.82 SEs on one of the lifts of their carrier. Notable are the many 'personal messages' of the crew, usually addressed to the Libyan leader. (USN)

Taken several years later, this close-up photograph of one of F/A-18As from VFA-131 that participated in attacks on Benghazi, shows a rare 'kill marking' for one of the Libyan SAM or radar sites knocked out on 15 April 1986. (Marc Chiabeau)

An F/A-18A from the VFA-132 Privateers loaded with drop tanks and AGM-88A HARM anti-radar missiles, being re-spotted on the deck of the USS *Coral Sea* prior to launch for attack on targets in the Benghazi area. (USN)

Intermingled wreckage of what was probably a Libyan Boeing 727 airliner and the rotor of a wrecked Mi-8 destroyed during the USN strike on Benina AB. (Albert Grandolini Collection)

The fin of a Libyan F.27 transport destroyed by USN A-6Es at Benina AB. The old Douglas C-47 in the background appears to have survived this attack with only some minor damage to the rear cabin. (Albert Grandolini Collection)

A formation of A-6E TRAM Intruders from VA-34 Blue Blasters – the squadron that bombed the Jamhuriya Barracks in Benghazi. (USN)

A post-strike reconnaissance photograph of Benina AB, taken by an SR-71A. Clearly visible is the wreckage of the destroyed F.27 transport and two Mi-8 helicopters, as well as a damaged Mi-8. The wreckage of several other destroyed aircraft and helicopters had already been removed by the time this photograph was taken. (USAF)

Post-Strike Dramas

By 0213 local time, all surviving fighter-bombers were back over the Mediterranean. F-14 Tomcats from USS *America* and several warships of the USN remained busy examining every F-111F and EF-111A that streamed north in order to prevent any LAAF interceptors from exploiting the post-strike chaos. At least one pair of MiG-25s is known to have been scrambled from Mitiga AB, but their pilots didn't attempt venturing over the sea. RIO Dave Parsons explained:

> The F-14s had a grand-stand view of all the fireworks and was hoping some Libyan interceptor would approach. But nothing happened so they deloused everybody coming out and stayed south until all packages recovered.

While all involved USN aircraft were safely back aboard the two aircraft carriers by 0253, the USAF strike package was going through the next drama. Most of the F-111Fs returning from the attack on Tripoli were desperately short of fuel. Puffy-11 was nearly shoved away from its tanker by another crew; Remit-31 had to do some 'torching' – dumping fuel and igniting it with the afterburner

The crew of this EA-6B Prowler from VAQ-135 Black Ravens hold their hands up as the 'brown shirts' – air wing quality control deck crew – of the USS *Coral Sea* perform last minute checks on their aircraft, prior to the start of another mission. VAQ-135 provided highly effective support for A-6E formations that bombed Benina and Jamhuriya Barracks on 15 April 1986. (USN)

– in order to mark the way for Elton-43, the crew of which was flying in complete darkness and without any other navigational aids but their stand-by compass. Eventually, despite lots of tension and critical situations, all surviving fighter-bombers and electronic warfare aircraft managed to hook-up before running out of fuel – although not necessarily on their assigned tankers. Contrary to what might be expected, the formation did not turn back home right away: for nearly an hour, it continued circling north-east of Tunisia, waiting to see if Karma-52 might reappear after all. Only then did Colonel Westbrook order all aircraft back to Britain. Even then, the USAF mission was still long from over, as the pilots still had to perform a gruelling, seven-hour flight back home by night, including another IFR-operation. While underway, the decision was taken to divert Elton-43 to NAS Rota in Spain.[54] All aircraft returned to their bases in Britain by 0810, ending a mission that lasted 14 hours and 35 minutes.

The activity of US aircraft did not cease immediately after the end of Operation El Dorado Canyon. While the two CVBGs of the USN took a defensive posture, they remained in the central

Less glamorous than most other aircraft involved in US operations against Libya in 1986, SH-3 Sea King helicopters of the USN attracted little public attention. It therefore remains little known that several of them received a camouflage pattern in tan and olive green: this was applied in case any US aircraft were shot down over the Libyan mainland and a SAR operation would be necessary. (Dave Parsons)

An SR-71A approaching a KC-135Q tanker for in-flight refuelling: at least five such operations – and up to 16 tanker aircraft – were required to support every Black-Bird mission over Libya. (USAF)

Mediterranean, just north of the Tripoli FIR. Meanwhile, Lockheed P-3C Orion MPA and one of two USN nuclear-powered attack submarines known to have been deployed off Libya at the time ran a search and rescue (SAR) operation for Karma-52. However, after finding no traces of the downed airmen or their aircraft, this was terminated at 1700.

Reconnaissance aircraft of the USAF continued operating along the Libyan borders – and sometimes within Libyan airspace too. The first attempt to collect post-strike reconnaissance was undertaken by two Lockheed SR-71A Black Birds during the morning of 15 April. The results of this mission were disappointing because of thick cloud cover over Tripoli and Benghazi. Two additional SR-71A made another high-speed pass on 16 April, but again without much success. Finally, during the third attempt on

17 April, both Black Birds brought back useful photographs after passing in a semi-circle over Benghazi and Tripoli. During this mission, the SR-71A piloted by Major Brian Shul was targeted by several SA-2s and SA-5s, prompting him to accelerate to Mach 3.45 – well above the aircraft's limit of Mach 3.2: probably the fastest any SR-71A ever flew.[55]

Table 7: USAF Aircraft involved in Post-Strike Reconnaissance over Libya, 1517 April 1986

Call-sign	Aircraft	Task & Notes
Finney 55	KC-135Q	support for SR-71A on 15 April
Finney 56	KC-10A	support for SR-71A on 15 April
Tromp 30	SR-71A	post-strike reconnaissance on 15 April
Tromp 31	SR-71A	post-strike reconnaissance on 15 April
Fatty 53	KC-135Q	support for SR-71A on 16 April
Fatty 54	KC-135Q	support for SR-71A on 16 April
Fatty 55	KC-135Q	support for SR-71A on 16 April
Lute 30	SR-71A	post-strike reconnaissance on 16 April
Lute 31	SR-71A	post-strike reconnaissance on 16 April
Minor 54	KC-135Q	support for SR-71A on 17 April
Minor 55	KC-135Q	support for SR-71A on 17 April
Minor 56	KC-10A	support for SR-71A on 17 April
Phony 30	SR-71A	post-strike reconnaissance on 17 April
Phony 31	SR-71A	post-strike reconnaissance on 17 April

CHAPTER 3
ITALIAN AFFAIRS

The Libyans were deeply shocked by the US air strikes on Tripoli and Benghazi. Bulgarian Ambassador Philip Ichpekov visited Gaddafi shortly after the strike to find a broken man, bitterly complaining he could not trust anyone. The Bulgarian answered that his country was always supportive and that all the Bulgarian personnel had been mobilized to treat the numerous wounded.[56] Of course, officially Tripoli acted as if not impressed at all, declaring a victory and to have shot down three US aircraft including an F-111F, the wreckage of which was supposedly recovered and would be turned to the USSR. Actually, the Libyans became so nervous that their air defences repeatedly opened fire for several nights, although no US aircraft operated over either Tripoli or Benghazi at the time.

After recovering his composure, the Libyan strongman was quick to order a retaliation. Around 1700 on 15 April, two SS-1c Scud-B surface-to-surface missiles were fired against the Italian island of Lampedusa – where the US Coast Guard ran a LORAN-C navigational station. Both missiles missed their target, crashing into the sea about 2km north-west and south-west of Cap Ponente. But the explosions were heard all over the island and shocked the local population.[57]

Ironically, about an hour after this attack, Washington warned Rome – and instantly announced the withdrawal of all US personnel from Lampedusa, 'for security reasons'. The departure of the Americans in turn caused collective panic among locals: amid wild rumours about additional detonations, low-flying aircraft and supposed Libyan warships approaching, some of the people preferred to leave their homes and seek security in one of the many bunkers left behind from the Second World War or in caves.

Craxi was furious about Gaddafi's 'betrayal': the Scud attack on Lampedusa caused a public outcry in Italy over the government's mismanagement of the entire affair with Libya. The next morning, the Italian Prime Minister summoned the Chief of Staff, General Riccardo Bisognero, and the Commander-in-Chief of the AMI, General Basillio Cottone, and ordered them to put the entire military on full war alert and develop plans for retaliation against Libya – including air strikes against selected targets in Tripoli and Benghazi! The AMI instantly cancelled all leave, recalled all personnel and began arming and refuelling all operational aircraft, preparing them for take-off at short notice. Some units were also prepared for deployment to air bases on Sicily. Interestingly, while the AMI reported a total strength of 40 F-104G and 126 F-104S Starfighters (with 54 F-104S-CB fighter-bombers and 72 F-104S-CIO interceptors), 54 Fiat G.91Rs and 36 Fiat G.91Ys as fully mission capable, its commanders selected the brand-new MRCA Tornados of the CLIV Gruppo/6th Stormo and CLVI Gruppo/36th Stormo for strikes against Libya. Their crews spent the next two weeks running intensive exercises at Gioia del

Colle and Trapani Air Bases, while the military began planning a combined aerial and amphibious assault to destroy Libyan Navy and a number of other targets along the coast.

On 16 April, the AMI launched Operation Girasole, within the frame of which defences on Lampedusa and Sicily were significantly bolstered. As one of the first measures, 12 additional F-104S from the XXI Gruppo of the 53rd Stormo redeployed from Trapani to NAS Sigonella, reinforcing 18 F-104S of the XVIII Gruppo already deployed there. All the Starfighters were re-armed with newly acquired AIM-9L Sidewinders. Although already available to the AMI, for unknown reasons such weapons were never installed on Italian interceptors before. In the rush caused by the Scud attack on Lampedusa, this task was accomplished in just one week. Even then, early during Operation Girasole, pilots scrambling with AIM-9L-armed Starfighters lacked necessary instructions, without the training that would enable them to deploy the new weapons. It took weeks to remedy all related problems and develop proper tactics. As well as Starfighters, the 134th Remote Radar Squadron deployed its AN/AFPS-8 radar to Lampedusa, where a new SIGINT station – the Operative Centre for Electronic Research (Centro Operativo Ricerca Elettronica) – was constructed.

The defences of Sicily were bolstered considerably too. Two new radar stations operated by the AMI were established near Crotone and Marsala, enabling the establishment of an air defence system including about 10,000 troops from all three branches of the Italian military, that covered the airspace of Sicily and Lampedusa.[58] Air defences were reinforced through the deployment of two SPADA SAM sites (one at Sigonella and another at Comiso, where it protected the US units equipped with nuclear-armed BGM-109G cruise missiles) and a MIM-23B I-HAWK SAM site of the Italian Army (deployed at Sigonella). Furthermore, a detachment consisting of several Tornados from the 61st Stormo and at least three Aermacchi MB.339As of the Lecce Air Academy was forward-deployed to the small airfield on Panteleria island, and readied for combat operations.[59]

Lockheed C-130H Hercules and G.222 military transports also began deploying to Lampedusa paratroopers of the 5th Airborne Battalion 'Folgore', the 1st Airborne Battalion 'Tuscania' and a company of Carabinieri on 16 April. This build-up was continued through the spring and summer with the help of requisitioned civilian airliners, the Italian Navy's amphibious ships and even requisitioned merchant ships escorted by six warships. AMI Starfighters flew 68 top cover sorties for this operation, for the protection of Atlantic MPAs that were patrolling the area and for the civilian transports involved. They also performed 70 operational scrambles, 450 hours of air defence operations and 108 hours of reconnaissance operations.

A reconstruction of 'Remit 31' – the first of nine F-111Fs (serial number 70-2390) planned to attack Bab al-Aziziya Compound in Tripoli on 15 April 1986, and one of only two to successfully release its four GBU-10E/B LGBs on that target. Unlike earlier (US-based) F-111-variants that wore camouflage colours with hard-edged patterns virtually identical between aircraft, UK-based examples received soft-edged patterns, only 'generally similar' between aircraft. Tail codes and national insignia were flat black. Except for wing insignia (applied on the left side of the fuselage, behind the cockpit), the fin-tip housing for ECM-systems painted in blue was the only marking identifying this aircraft as assigned to the 495th TFS. Weeks after the Tripoli raid, 70-2390 received a small white bomb marking – shaped similar to the 'Fat Man' nuclear bomb – on the left side of the fuselage, just in front and slightly below the bottom front corner of the escape capsule.

A reconstruction of 'Puffy 11', the first F-111F (serial number 71-0893) to take off from RAF Lakenheath for Operation El Dorado Canyon, and the only to successfully bomb Tripoli IAP with 12 Mk.82 AIR (carried on BRU-3A/A multiple ejector racks). Like other Aardvarks of the 48th TFW, it wore no special markings, except for its fin-tip painted in blue, identifying it as assigned to the 492nd TFS. Like all other 48th TFW F-111Fs, the last three digits of the tail number were stencilled in white on the front bottom corner of both nose wheel doors. Pilot and crew chief names were painted in white on the left nose gear door, while the WSO and assistant crew chief names were on the right. It was only several months after this operation that one kind of special marking often wrongly associated with the Libya raid began to appear – but then on all aircraft of the 48th TFW, regardless if they had been involved in that operation or not. This was a retention of the Second World War North African Campaign ribbon. Such a marking was retained by most F-111Fs at least until they were transferred to Cannon AB in 1991.

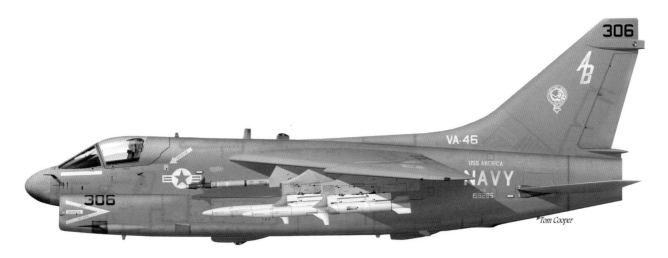

A reconstruction of one of eight A-7Es from VA-46 Clansmen known to have supported USAF raids on Tripoli during the night of 14/15 April 1986. As usual at the time, it was painted in the so-called 'tactical paint scheme' (TPS) consisting of Dark Ghost Gray (FS 36320) on upper surfaces and sides, over Light Ghost Gray (FS36375) on undersurfaces. After several weeks of intensive operations off Libya, in late March 1986, the TPS began showing the usual signs of wear. The aircraft is illustrated as configured during Operation El Dorado Canyon, armed with four AGM-88 HARM anti-radar missiles and a pair of AIM-9L Sidewinders for self-defence.

The first of two USN squadrons equipped with F/A-18A Hornets and assigned to the USS *Coral Sea*-embarked CVW-14 was VFA-131 Wildcats, the aircraft of which wore modex in the range 100114. As usual, all were painted in a standardized TPS consisting of Dark Ghost Gray (FS 36320) over Light Ghost Gray (FS36375), but otherwise only a bare minimum of unit insignia. Nearly half of the VFA-131 was involved in attacks on targets in the Benghazi area on 15 April, flying CAPs but also SEAD sorties as cover for involved A-6E Intruders.

The second USN squadron embarked onboard USS *Coral Sea* and equipped with F/A-18As was VFA-132 Privateers. While all Hornets of this unit wore the usual TPS, some appear to have had a slightly more accented 'anti-glare panel' applied in dark grey in front of the cockpit, with very soft and often rough edges. As usual at that time, unit insignia was kept at a bare minimum and toned down. The aircraft is shown configured with two each of AIM-7 Sparrows, AIM-9 Sidewinders and Mk.20 Rockeye CBUs –while flying a surface combat air patrol during Operation Attain Document III/Prairie Fire in late March 1986.

A reconstruction of the A-6E modex AK502 (BuAerNo 161681), assigned to the VA-55 Sea Horses – a squadron that saw much action during Operations Attain Document I/II/III, Prairie Fire and El Dorado Canyon. Unsurprisingly, this resulted in the application of numerous kill markings on its Intruders. In the case of AK502, these included a kill marking for a Libyan Nanuchka-class corvette during an action on 25 March 1986, and one for a Libyan MiG-23 fighter destroyed at Benina AB on 15 April 1986. Otherwise, and as usual, this A-6E was painted in the TPS, but by mid-April 1986 this was not only badly worn and repeatedly corrected to fight corrosion, but also some parts of the airframe – most notably the radome – were replaced and not repainted.

The Jaguar A c/n A100, coded 11-MP, was officially assigned to the EC 2/11 Vosges (insignia shown in the inset) and flown by Lieutenant Guy Wurtz during anti-radar attacks on 6 and 7 January 1986. The aircraft is shown as configured during that mission, with one Martel ADAM under the centreline. ADAM stood for 'Auto Directeur Amélioré' (Improved Automatic Direction Finder), and was actually an improved seeker-head, enabling the missile to target radars working in all three bands (L, S and C): previously, three different variants of Martel were necessary, each of which covered one of the bands in question. Other equipment included two RP.35 drop tanks on inboard underwing pylons, a Barracuda ECM-pod on the outboard left pylon and (not shown here) a Phimat chaff & flare dispenser on the outboard right pylon.

Escadre de Chasse 5 provided most Mirage F.1Cs operated in Chad in 1986–1987. As usual since their service entry, all were painted in blue-grey (FS 35164) on top surfaces and sides, and silver on undersurfaces. Except for unit insignia applied on the fin – in this case that of EC.1/5 Vendée – and a few personalized RP.35 drop tanks, no special insignia is known to have been applied on any of these aircraft. Armament consisted of a pair each of Matra Super 530F-1 (on LM.38 underwing pylons) and Matra R.550 Magic Mk.1. Inset is the official patch of EC.1/5, including traditional markings of three of its flights: SPA.26 Cigogne, C.46 Trident and SPA.124 Jeanne d'Arc.

The crucial third member of the triad of French combat aircraft deployed in Chad in 19861987 was the Breguet Br.1150 Atlantic. Although designed as an anti-submarine and maritime patrol aircraft, and operated by Aéronavale (French Naval aviation), it was deployed for numerous other roles in Chad, ranging from makeshift early warning aircraft to ELINT/SIGINT-gatherer. Camouflage colours consisted of azure blue on top surfaces and flat white on lower surfaces and sides, while national insignia was worn in four positions only. Most Atlantics deployed in 1986 and 1987 were drawn from the Flottille 23F, but were manned by different crews, including those from Flottille 22F and 23F. While all regularly carried Barracuda ECM-pods for self-defence, installed under the port wing, serial number 53 was one of two aircraft from the 23F (the other was 67) known to have been modified to deploy AS.37 Martel anti-radar missiles in 1987. Inset are the insignia of 21F (left) and 23F.

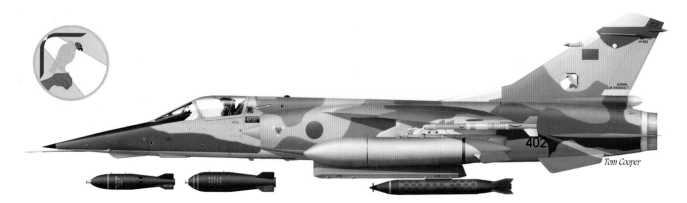

Camouflaged in standardized pattern consisting of sand (similar to 30266), medium olive green (FS 34127) and purple brown (FS 30099) on top surfaces, and light grey (similar to 36375) on undersurfaces, Mirage F.1ADs of No. 1012 Squadron LAAF saw intensive action over northern Chad in 1986 and 1987, when they were primarily deployed for ground attack, armed with a wide range of French-made bombs. Among these were 400kg SAMP Type 25E2/1 (lower left corner) and SAMP Type 21C (centre), but also sophisticated BLG-66 Belouga CBUs (usually carried in pairs on the 'surfboard' installed under the centreline; sometimes also on outboard underwing pylons). Inset is the insignia of No. 1012 Squadron.

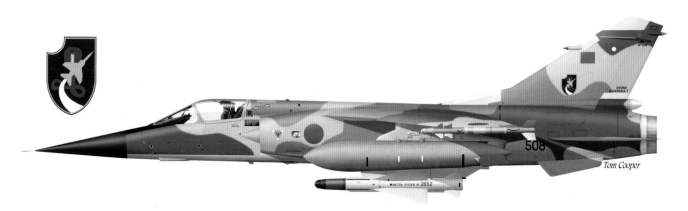

Libyan Mirage F.1ED interceptors wore the same camouflage pattern as F.1ADs and national insignia in six positions. Serials on both variants were applied in black on the rear fuselage. Armed with old, difficult to use and unreliable Matra R.530F air-to-air missiles (shown under the centreline) and more modern Matra R.550 Magic Mk.1s, LAAF Mirage F.1EDs flew a relatively small number of CAPs over northern Chad. More often, they were deployed for ground-attack sorties. Inset is the insignia of No. 1015 Squadron, including a green cobra and a yellow Mirage (the insignia of the MiG-23BN-equipped No. 1070 Squadron was quite similar, but included a map of Libya in green and a yellow silhouette of a MiG-23.)

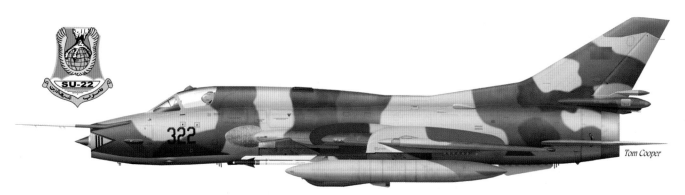

Most Libyan Su-22s, Su-22Ms and Su-22M-3Ks were originally painted in beige (BS381C/388) and olive green (BS381C/298) on top surfaces and sides, and light admiralty grey (BS381C/637) on undersurfaces prior to delivery. Upon delivery, the top-side camouflage pattern was darkened through the addition of dark olive green (possibly black olive, RAL6015). Serials were applied differently, with some aircraft receiving the last four of their construction number in Arabic digits; others (like this Su-22M-3K) the last three in European digits; and some Soviet-style 'bort' numbers. Primarily deployed as fighter-bombers in Chad, they were usually armed with FAB-500M-54, FAB-250M-62 or FAB-500M-62 GP bombs, or various CBUs, such as RBK-250s. Whenever activity of French aircraft in the combat zone was reported, R-13M air-to-air missiles were installed on inboard underwing pylons. Inset is the insignia of No. 1032 Squadron, which moved to Woutia AB in the late 1980s.

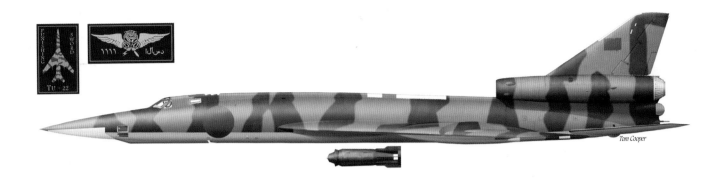

Libyan Tu-22s wore the same camouflage pattern in grey-green (BS381C/283) and dark green (BS381C/641) or black olive (RAL6015), like examples delivered to Iraq. Theoretically, this pattern was standardized, but there were significant differences in its application between aircraft. Heavy maintenance work around engines resulted in frequent reapplication of camouflage colours in that area and on the fin. National markings were applied in six positions, while four-digit serials were worn in black, Arabic digits, on the cover of the front undercarriage bay only. Inset are the 'wing patch' worn by Libyan Tu-22 crews and the insignia of No. 1111 Squadron, LAAF, as well as a FAB-1500M-54 bomb as frequently deployed by this type in Chad.

A reconstruction of one of about 20 MiG-23MFs which Libya received in 1984–1986. The type was camouflaged in a standardized pattern consisting of beige (BS381C/388), dark brown (BS381C/411 or 450, similar to FS 20095) and olive green (BS381C/298, similar to FS 34098) on the upper surfaces, and light admiralty grey (BS381C/697, FS35622) on undersurfaces. Dielectric panels were usually painted in medium grey (FS26152), but – like earlier MiG-23MSs – a number of LAAF MiG-23MFs had their radomes painted in white. The aircraft arrived armed with R-23R and R-23T medium-range air-to-air missiles (shown installed underwing) and R-60MK, short-range missiles, but were modified for deployment of much more potent R-24R/T missiles too. When flying CAPs over northern Chad, they frequently used drop tanks: these could be installed under wings swept fully forward only, and had to be ejected before the aircraft could accelerate.

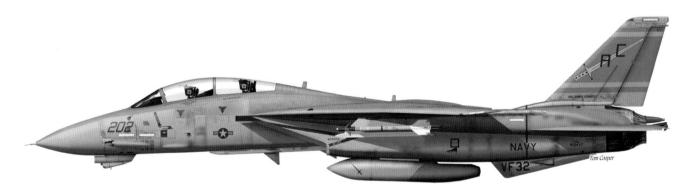

A reconstruction of the F-14A modex AC202 – BuAerNo 159437 – as flown by Lieutanant Hermon C. Cook III and Lieutenant Commander Steven Patrick Collins, when they shot down a Libyan MiG-23MF on 4 January 1989. The aircraft wore the standardized TPS consisting of Dark Ghost Gray (FS 36320) over Light Ghost Gray (FS36375), and was armed with four AIM-7 Sparrows (the exact mix between older AIM-7Fs and AIM-7Ms remains unknown) and two AIM-9M Sidewinders. It is illustrated with the kill marking that was originally applied: this was removed and replaced by a small Libyan flag, applied on the cockpit rail, right behind the name of the RIO by the time USS John F. Kennedy returned from that memorable cruise.

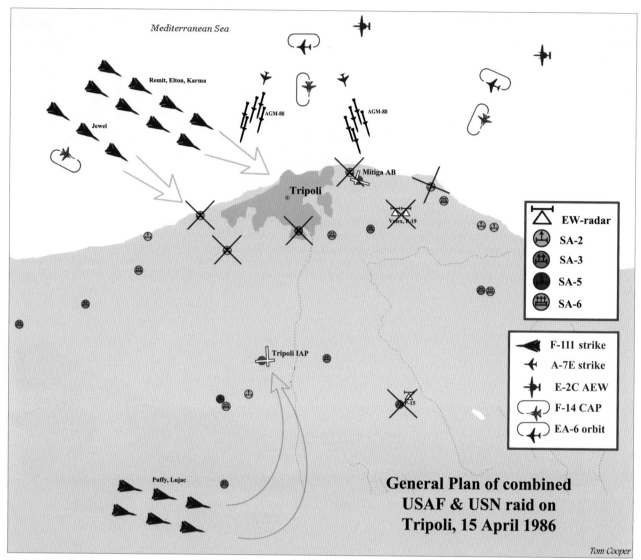

Mediterranean Sea

Remit, Elton, Karma

Jewel

AGM-88

AGM-88

Tripoli

Mitiga AB

Vmex, F-19

Tripoli IAP

F-15

Puffy, Lujac

	EW-radar
	SA-2
	SA-3
	SA-5
	SA-6

	F-111 strike
	A-7E strike
	E-2C AEW
	F-14 CAP
	EA-6 orbit

**General Plan of combined
USAF & USN raid on
Tripoli, 15 April 1986**

Tom Cooper

An EF-111A of the 42nd ECS: four of these highly sophisticated aircraft for electronic warfare provided stand-off jamming for the F-111Fs that attacked Tripoli. Combined with AGM-88 HARMs fired by the USN's A-7Es, electronic countermeasures emitted by them proved highly effective in suppressing most of the Libyan air defences. (Albert Grandolini Collection)

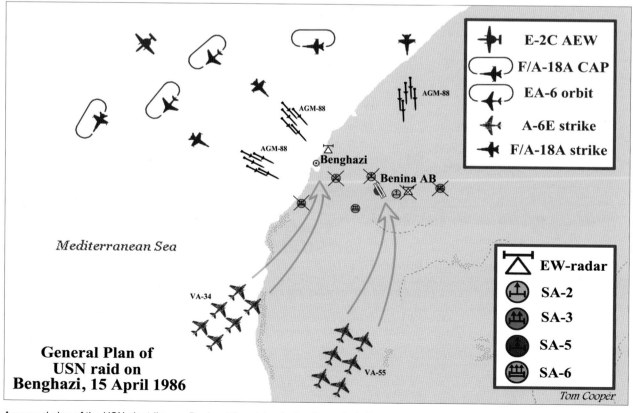

AGM-88

AGM-88

AGM-88

Benghazi

Benina AB

Mediterranean Sea

VA-34

VA-55

	E-2C AEW
	F/A-18A CAP
	EA-6 orbit
	A-6E strike
	F/A-18A strike

	EW-radar
	SA-2
	SA-3
	SA-5
	SA-6

**General Plan of
USN raid on
Benghazi, 15 April 1986**

Tom Cooper

A general plan of the USN air strikes on Benina AB and Jamhuriya Barracks in Benghazi on 15 April 1986, with the known positions of Libyan SAM sites. (Tom Cooper)

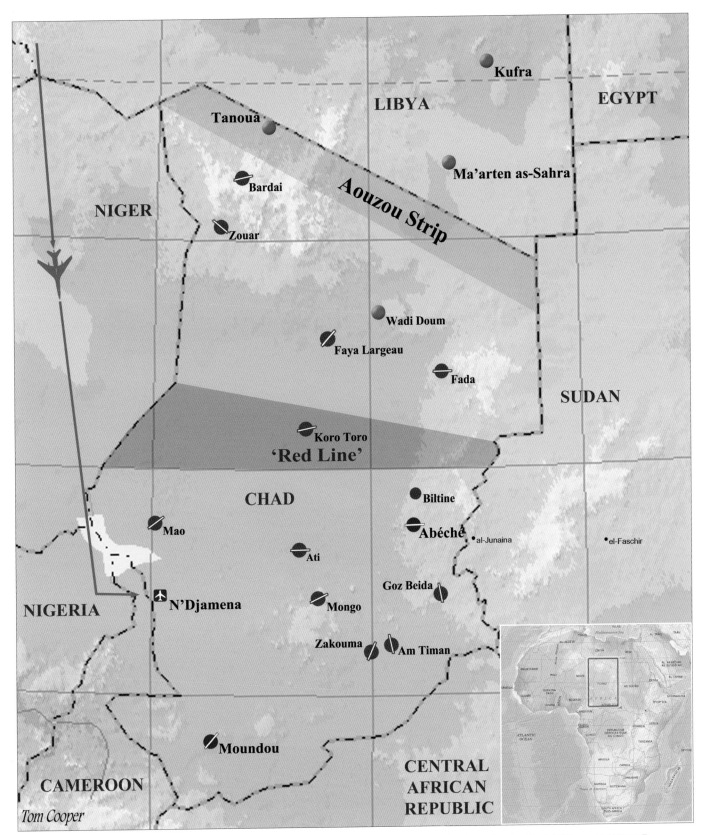

A map of Chad, with the approximate route taken by the LAAF Tu-22 that was shot down while attempting to attack N'Djamena IAP on 7 September 1987. (Tom Cooper)

A pair of F-111Es (from the 77th TFS) and a single EF-111A (from the 42nd ECS) during in-flight refuelling from a KC-135A tanker. Good coordination between tankers and fighter-bombers proved essential for the success of long-range operations by F-111s. (USAF)

While taken over the Bardenas Reales range in Spain, several years later, this photograph of an F-111F releasing Mk.82 AIRs nicely illustrates the method by which 'Puffy-11' delivered its attack on Tripoli IAP: flying at high speed (note the vapour above the wings, which usually appears when the aircraft is approaching supersonic speed) and low altitude, while the Pave Tack 'head' at the bottom of the aircraft is tracking the target. The ALQ-131 ECM-pod is installed underneath the engine nacelles. (USAF)

As one of the final parts of preparation for the Italian retaliation against Libya, a single AMI RF-104G reconnaissance fighter should have made a high-speed dash over Tripoli, collecting up-to-date intelligence, at an unknown date. Whether such a mission was actually flown or not, the Libyans appear not to have detected any of these deployments. Their only Italy-related reaction after the Scud attack on Lampedusa was for Libyan intelligence to collect all Italian personnel that served in the country, bring them to Tripoli and interrogate them for about ten days. The Libyans were especially curious to find out who informed the Italians about the incoming US attack, prompting them to evacuate Benina AB. Eventually, all Italian personnel were repatriated on Gaddafi's personal order.

Italian military preparations are said to have continued until the cancellation of the actual strike, only few minutes before it was due to start, at an unknown date. Supposedly, the primary reasons were complaints from AMI commanders that their aircraft would suffer heavy losses due to the lack of suitable ECM equipment, along with expectations of massive collateral damage. However,

it seems that the actual reason for the cancellation of this strike was over doubts expressed by General Cottone over the nature of Libyan Scud attacks, that made Craxi believe that he had been hoaxed by the Americans into getting involved in their feud with Gaddafi. Cottone observed that satellite intelligence of launching pads for Libyan Scuds showed nothing and that his deputy, General Mario Arpino – who was present at the headquarters of NATO's 5th Allied Tactical Air Force (ATAF) in Vicenza – reported no warning about an incoming Scud strike. Finally, Italian Navy warships deployed around Lampedusa found no traces of any kind of missiles.

The fact that the Libyan ambassador to Rome subsequently made an ambiguous statement about his country firing two Scuds, 'against American forces only, not against Italian people', appears to have been considered irrelevant. Nevertheless, all the training, rehearsals and planning of the Italian armed forces during the period April-July had not been for nothing: the resulting plans were subsequently continuously upgraded, 'just in case of another hot-headed action of Gaddafi'.[60]

The Libyan Scud attack on Lampedusa prompted the Italian military into a hurried effort to upgrade its overall capabilities. One of the resulting measures was the introduction of the then latest AIM-9L Sidewinder all-aspect air-to-air missiles, four of which can be seen on this pair of F-104Ss cruising high above the port of Palermo on Sicily. Noe the 'toned-down' serials, introduced around the same time. (Albert Grandolini Collection)

An RF-104G of the AMI in the mid-1980s. According to unconfirmed reports, one of these reconnaissance fighters flew a high-speed sortie over the Tripoli area in 1986. (Albert Grandolini Collection)

Left: A trio of then brand-new Tornado interdiction-strike fighters of the 36th Stormo – the unit selected to lead Italian air strikes against Libya in 1986 – reportedly cancelled only minutes before they were due to start.
(Albert Grandolini Collection)

Bottom left: The crisis with Libya in mid-1986 prompted not only a comprehensive modernization and reinforcement of Italian defensive and offensive capabilities towards Libya, but also caused the AMI to run some very realistic exercises. Here, a group of ordnancemen in full NBC (nuclear, biological, chemical) gear can be seen loading a Hunting BL.755 CBU on an F-104 Starfighter, parked inside a hardened aircraft shelter.
(Albert Grandolini Collection)

Below: A trio of G.222 transports of the AMI: they were heavily utilized during the deployment of additional Italian Army troops to Lampedusa in April and May 1986.
(Albert Grandolini Collection)

Three MB.339A light strikers – all armed with gun-pods and carrying drop tanks –inside an underground shelter on Panteleria island in 1986.
(Albert Grandolini Collection)

Libyan Ballistic Missiles

Searching for arms that would enable a direct confrontation with Israel, during the mid-1970s Gaddafi began acquiring surface-to-surface missiles from the USSR. In 1976, Libya purchased about a dozen 9K72E Elbrus-E systems (ASCC-code SS-1c Scud-B), including a similar number of MAZ-543/9P117 Uragan transporter-erector-launchers (TELs) and 80 R-17E (Scud-B) missiles with a range of 450km. Two years later, an order was made for approximately 45 Soviet-made 9K53 Luna-M (ASCC-code FROG-7) rockets with a range of 70km .

Subsequent Libyan orders brought the total of 9P117 TELs to 72 and the number of R-17E missiles to between 200 and 300, enabling the establishment of six battalions (each with 12 TELs) controlled by four missile brigades.

Iranian Episode

It is somewhat ironic that despite tensions and low intensity conflicts with nearly all of its neighbours and many foreign powers, Libyan Scuds were to see their first combat service in Iran, and then against another Arab country.

In 1984, the war between Iran and Iraq had developed into a stalemate. Following Iraqi advances into south-western Iran early in the war, the Iranians mobilized their forces and counter-attacked, causing heavy casualties to the invader. Starting in summer 1982, they began launching ever larger offensives aimed at capturing Basra, the second largest city in Iraq. Two of their major offensives north of Basra, in spring 1983 and 1984, nearly broke the back of the Iraqi military, but eventually failed. Baghdad's offer of a cease-fire and negotiations were repeatedly refused by Tehran, which insisted on continuing the war until the fall of the Iraqi government of Saddam Hussein at-Tikriti. In an attempt to weaken the Iranian economy, the Iraqi government ordered its air force to bomb Iranian cities and industrial complexes, and – in April 1984 – began using Scuds to hit the Iranian petrochemical complex near the port of Bandar-e Khomeini.

Because the Islamic Republic of Iran Air Force (IRIAF) was severely depleted by combat attrition from the initial years of the war with Iraq, it could not hit back strongly and thus the Iranians began searching for alternatives. This is when they obtained their first batch of Scud missiles from Libya and Syria.

One of biggest secrets of the Iran-Iraq War was that Iran had obtained its first Scuds directly from the Soviet Union in the 1970s. At the time, Iran was a close ally of the USA and Israel, and the government of Shah Reza Mohammed Pahlavi attempted to enter cooperation with the latter in a project to develop an advanced variant of the French-designed Dassault MD.620 missile, designated Jericho in Israeli service. When the Israelis proved reluctant to cooperate, the Iranians turned to Moscow instead and ordered 18 9P117 TELs and 36 R-17E missiles from them in 1977. A base for these systems was constructed north of Khorramabad and was nearly 80 percent complete, but only eight launchers and

A pair of heavy MAZ-543/9P117 Uragan TELs with R-17E (SS-1c Scud-B) missiles during a parade in Tripoli in the mid-1980s. (Albert Grandolini Collection)

Three of the 45 9K53 Luna-M systems acquired by Libya in the 1970s. Libyans expended 114 such ballistic missiles in Chad in 1987. (Tom Cooper Collection)

One of the two MAZ-543/9P117 TELs provided by Libya to Iran, seen on the streets of Tehran in 1986. (Tom Cooper Collection)

Together with two TELs, Libya provided 20 R-17E missiles to Iran. The Qattam al-Omniya Brigade of the Islamic Revolutionary Guard Corps fired all of them against Iraq, primarily Baghdad, which is rather ironic as the Arabs of Libya were supplying missiles for a Persian nation to use against another Arab country. (Tom Cooper Collection)

few missiles were delivered by the time of the revolution that toppled the Shah in February 1979.

The Khorramabad base and all the weapons there were subsequently abandoned. Indeed, the new government in Tehran initially banned procurement and use of ballistic missiles. But a few years later, there was a dramatic change. Confronted with ever more intensive Iraqi use of R-17Es, in late 1984 Tehran ordered the engineer Mohsen Rafigh-Doost to make the existing Scuds operational again, obtain additional missiles and have IRGC (Islamic Revolutionary Guard Corps) personnel trained abroad to operate the system. While the Iranians were undergoing training, Syrian specialists helped Iran to refurbish their Scuds and TELs. Furthermore, Libya provided two 9P117s and 20 R-17Es. Thus came into being the IRGC's Khatam al-Anbya Missile Force that subsequently played a prominent

role in the so-called 'War of the Cities' for the rest of Iran-Iraq War.

Iranian-Libyan cooperation did not end there. When – in response to IRGC Scud attacks on Baghdad – the Iraqis began bombing Tehran with the help of Soviet-made MiG-25RBs, the IRIAF deputed Colonel Mustafa Ardestani – one of its top pilots – to Libya, where he test-flew the MiG-25 in 1985.[61]

Indigenous Projects

Because the Libyans were never satisfied with Soviet-made Scuds, Gaddafi meanwhile began searching for alternative sources of similar weapons. In 1980, Tripoli contracted the German company Orbital Transport und Raketen AG (Orbital Transport and Rockets Inc., OTRAG) to develop a missile infrastructure in Libya. Under US pressure, OTRAG ceased its cooperation with Tripoli in 1982, but most of its personnel and equipment remained in the country. By 1987, a team of experts led by German missile engineer Walter Ziegler enabled the Libyans to integrate remnants of the OTRAG project into the programme code-named Ittisalt, based at a research centre near the Siwa Oasis. The aim of this project was to develop a liquid-fuelled missile with a range of 300-700km. Around the same time, the Libyans negotiated for the transfer of knowledge from several Brazilian firms, and it seems that some of this found its way into the project for a medium-range ballistic missile named al-Fatah. Over time, three major related facilities were constructed: a solid propellant plant and rocket engine test stand at Tarhuna; the al-Fajer Alga Did factory for maintenance and modifications of R-17E missiles; and the refurbishment plant for liquid-fuelled rocket engines run by the Central Organization for Electronic Research in Tripoli. Nevertheless, the entire project suffered from poor management and over-reliance on assistance from abroad. Both test-firings of al-Fatah missiles (one in 1987 and another in 1993) failed dismally.

Because of such problems, Libya subsequently concentrated on merely maintaining its existing inventory of Scud-B missiles. During the 1990s, they not only signed several contracts and agreements with Iraq, Iran, China and North Korea, but also continued smuggling related technology – including components for Scud missiles – using a number of front companies. That, however, is a story to be told at some other time.

CHAPTER 4
TOYOTA WARS

The Libyans barely found time to recover from the blows delivered by US military power in March and April 1986, before they found themselves confronted with a rapidly deteriorating position in Chad. The quick defeat of the fourth Libyan military intervention in that country, in February 1986, resulted in deepening rifts between Gaddafi and his Chadian allies, grouped within the Transitional National Government (Gouverment d'Union Nationale de Transition, GUNT), led by Goukouni Oueddei. By November that year, this organization was in tatters, leaving Libya without a Chadian proxy that could continue waging the war against the government of President Hissene Habré and his National Armed Forces of Chad (Forces Armées Nationales du Tchad, FANT).

Worse still, though unnoticed on the battlefield until it was much too late, the combination of strikes by the US military and clandestine operations of US and other Western intelligence

agencies had fundamentally shaken Gaddafi's rule over Libya. Indirectly, this had negative repercussions by badly weakening the general combat effectiveness of the Libyan military. In reaction to several actual and supposed coup attempts from 1984 and 1985, and then the failure in the face of US strikes, the Libyan leader greatly decreased funding and imposed strict limitations upon his military, greatly hindering not only its further growth but also its organization and function. Internal intelligence and security services proliferated and separated individual military units from each other: suspected of a possible lack of loyalty, even elite Army and Air Force units were left without funding and de-facto locked inside their bases through much of 1986. Therefore, after years of massive investment into education and training of entire new generations of Libyan officers and non-commissioned officers (NCOs) – and at the time all such efforts were about to start showing their first results Gaddafi forbade the establishment of division and wing-sized formations and commands, stopped the build-up of the Air Defence Command and curbed further growth of the regular Army.

Instead, he created the Jamhuriya Guard, a kind of praetorian guard responsible for the protection of Gaddafi, his family and

A rare photograph of a Libyan MiG-23BN fighter-bomber, about 30 of which saw intensive service during the fighting in Chad in 1986–1987. (via Pit Weinert)

A LAAF CH-47C (serial 016) near the village of Aouzou, in northern Chad, in early 1987. (Albert Grandolini Collection)

A LAAF pilot in front of his Mirage F.1ED. These interceptors were deployed during the last year of fighting in Chad: while it is known that they flew numerous combat air patrols, sometimes in coordination with pairs of MiG-23MSs and MiG-23MFs, no details are available about any of these. Note the relatively rare Matra R.530 air-to-air missile installed under the centreline. (via Pit Weinert)

The pilot of a LAAF Mirage (note the squadron patch on the right shoulder) in front of a LAAF Mi-8 at Wadi Doum AB, sometime in 1986. (via Pit Weinert)

his rule, staffed by loyal members of his clan and tribe. Better trained than the regular Army, they were equipped with modern T-72 MBTs, BMP-1 infantry-fighting vehicles (IFVs), multiple rocket launch systems (MRLS), Soviet-made 2S1 and 2S3 and Italian-made Palmaria self-propelled howitzers, ZSU-23-4 Shilka self-propelled anti-aircraft guns and even 9K33 Osa (ASCC-code SA-8 Gecko) self-propelled SAMs. Over the following years, the Jamhuriya Guard was increased in size to an equivalent of four mechanized brigades.

Despite such issues, the Libyan expeditionary force deployed in Chad was still impressive. It totalled about 8,000 troops organized into an equivalent of four brigades, supported by 300 MBTs, 200 IFVs, MRLS and heavy artillery. The LAAF usually maintained a presence of about 90 combat aircraft and helicopters deployed at air bases in southern Libya and northern Chad. There was at least one squadron of MiG-21s based at Kufra AB, and an equivalent of one squadron each of Aero L-39 Albatross light strikers, Mi-8 transport helicopters, Mi-25 helicopter gunships, MiG-23BNs, Mirage 5Ds, Mirage F.1s and SF.260s distributed between Tanoua AB (near Aouzou), Wadi Doum AB and Ma'arten as-Sahra AB.

New Times in Chad

As described in Part 2 of this mini-series, Chadian President Habré – who in 1986 controlled only the southern part of the country, below the 16th Parallel (the so-called 'Red Line') – spent most of the period between 1983 and 1986 rearming and reorganizing his military. Thanks to his far-sighted policy of not alienating but attracting and rewarding defections from his internal opponents, and the provision of significant military aid from France and the USA – which furnished an additional US$10 million in March and April 1986 – he was in a unique position to transform the FANT into an entirely new fighting force.

Contrary to what might have been expected, Habré turned down all Western offers of tanks, APCs and heavy artillery. Instead, relying on the advice of a cadre of his seasoned commanders – about two dozen of whom underwent training at various military schools in France and elsewhere in the West – he decided to spend most of his foreign military aid purchasing large numbers of Toyota 4WDs (four-wheel drive) and a plentiful supply of automatic firearms, anti-tank and anti-aircraft weapons, and related ammunition. FANT commanders like Hassan Djamous, Idris Deby, Ahmed Gorou and Mohammad Nouri became vocal proponents of reintroducing the traditional desert warfare of rapid movement and concentration, as practiced in ages past by Toubou and Zaghawa warriors. Their conclusion was that not only would their fighters find it easier to adapt to warfare against a modern military power like that of Libya, but that high speed and flexibility of operations combined with modern, yet simple armament could also overcome Libyan superiority in armour and firepower.

Indeed, the combination of fast 4WD pick-up trucks with modern anti-armour and anti-aircraft weapons (known as technicals), and their availability in large numbers – all supported

by a good logistics system, primarily run by French officers – promised to offer opportunities not only at tactical, but even at an operational level. It enabled Chadians to develop a force that optimized speed, manoeuvrability and firepower; that was able to dart around the battlefield, avoid exposing itself to superior Libyan firepower, then outflank Libyan armour and saturate it with swarming attacks from multiple sides at once. The same practice could obviously be applied for overcoming Libyan fortifications. Therefore, the FANT operated only two companies of light armoured vehicles – equipped with French-made Panhard AML-90 and Cadillac V-150 armoured cars – for additional fire-power during this period. The majority of about 28,000 of its troops were assigned to units equipped with the 4WD technicals.[62]

French advisors were important for successful operations by the Chadian Air Force (Armée de l'Air Tchadienne), re-established in 1984 and equipped with four C-130s (donated by the USA), three Douglas C-47s, one Douglas DC-4, one CASA C.212 and two Pilatus PC-7 trainers. Commanded by Captain Mornadji Mbaissanabe, this small force had only about 200 officers and other ranks. It was not only heavily dependent on French support for maintenance: few of its pilots were Chadians, while many were French and Zairians.

For air defences, the FANT was only equipped with relatively few old FIM-43A Red Eye man-portable air defence systems (MANPADs), provided by the Americans, and a handful of similar Strela-2 (ASCC-code SA-7 Grail) captured from Libyans. Therefore, they remained dependent on external support. The French not only provided interceptors and fighter-bombers that would patrol along the 'Red Line' in order to prevent the LAAF from venturing south of it, but also air defences for major military bases further south. Moreover, FANT ground units were reinforced by several teams (between 25 and 30 operators in total) from the 11th Shock Parachute Regiment (11e Régiment Parachutiste de Choc) equipped with modern, US-made FIM-92A Stinger MANPADs. Colloquially known as the 11e Choc, this unit was actually not part of the French Army, but a detachment of the DGSE's 'Operational Service' (Service Action), which operated in cooperation with a team from the 1st Marine Parachute Regiment (Régiment Parachutiste d'Infanterie de Marine, 1er RPIMa). Finally, a SIGINT-gathering team from the newly established 54th Communications Regiment (Régiment de Transmissions, 54e RT), including several Arab linguists, was assigned to the FANT HQ.[63]

On its arrival in Chad as part of Operation Épervier, starting in mid-February 1986, the French military showed a number of other innovations. Unlike Operation Manta in 1983, the overall size of the French Army contingent remained limited to about 1,400 troops. The French units were still primarily drawn from the 9th Marine Infantry Division (9e division d'Infanterie de Marine, 9e DIMa) and 11th Parachute Division (11e Division Parachutiste), but their training and equipment were different. They were deployed in small contingents of specialized troops equipped with high technology armament and sensors, primarily used to

Showing why the last phase of the Chadian War became known as 'Toyota Wars', this photograph shows long rows of Toyota 4WDs, modified as 'technicals' by the FANT through the addition of various heavy machine guns, light anti-aircraft cannons and guided anti-tank missiles. (via Pit Weinert)

bolster and secure a number of important FANT strongpoints along the Red Line, and few major bases further south. Instead of becoming directly involved in fighting for the Chadians, French forces generally played a supportive role. This was particularly obvious with the French Air Force(AdA), which was to operate more vividly – but also in an entirely different fashion – than ever before.

For most of 1986, the AdA contingent in Chad included about a dozen Jaguar A fighter-bombers and up to six Mirage F.1C interceptors from various units, with a few Mirage F.1CR tactical reconnaissance fighters of the 33rd Reconnaissance Wing (Escadre de Reconnaissance 33, ER.33), based at N'Djamena IAP.[64] Like earlier, two Atlantic MPAs were also usually deployed at N'Djamena. By 1987, they were equipped for a host of modifications, making them capable of serving as airborne command posts, conducting photo reconnaissance (with the help of the Omera 35 underwing pod) and as ELINT/SIGINT-gatherers (with the Arar 11, ALR-8 and APA-69 systems). At least two Atlantics were adapted for deployment of AS.37 Martel anti-radar missiles. For self-protection, they were usually equipped with one Barracuda ECM pod installed under the left wing.

At least one – but more often up to three – AdA Boeing C-135F tankers were present at N'Djamena too, together with 25 Transall C.160NG (Nouvelle Generation – new generation) that were operational by that time. Equipped with new avionics and navigational equipment, increased internal fuel capacity and an IFR-probe, the latter proved capable of flying non-stop to any French base overseas. Furthermore, 10 of the C-160NGs were equipped for easy conversion to aerial tankers, thus significantly bolstering the otherwise small French tanker fleet.

French air defences in Chad were also reinforced. The entire 403rd Artillery Regiment of the French Army (Régiment d'Artillerie, 403e RA), equipped with six triple launchers of US-made MIM-23B I-HAWK SAMs (12 missiles were ready to fire and six as back-up) and one Crotale SAM site (eight missiles ready for action and four as back-up), was protecting N'Djamena. Another Crotale SAM site – supported by Stinger-armed teams was deployed at Abéche. SAMs were complemented by a battery of six 20mm twin anti-aircraft cannons and two Chadian batteries equipped with 37mm and 40mm anti-aircraft cannons. Most importantly the French set up a radar centre in Moussoro (at the same site used during Operation Manta). Centred around a SNERI Centaure radar (Sociéte Nouvelle Electronique et Radio Industrie), with a range of about 193km (120 miles), it was operated by the AdA. It was protected by infantry of the 2nd Marine Infantry Regiment (Régiment d'Infanterie de Marine, 2e RIMA) and one of the 1e RIMA's Stinger teams. Sergeant Thierry Bourdil, who arrived there in May 1986, recalled:

Four or five days after my arrival, our protection was taken over by the 2nd Infantry Regiment of the Foreign Legion [Régiment Etranger d'Infanterie, 2e REI; authors' note]. We were all very busy because of constant flights by C.160s, which were delivering all the arms for the 2e REI: we had to guide them in order to ascertain a safe landing and a quick turn-around and take-off.

Mirage F.1CRs from ER.33 were a new feature in Chad of 1986. This example – coded 33-NA – was photographed from a Boeing C-135F tanker, while configured with two drop tanks, a Baracuda ECM-pod and R.550 Magic Mk.1 AAMs. (Jean-Pierre Gabriel)

A pair of Jaguars from EC.4/11 and a Mirage F.1C interceptor from EC.5, refuelling from a C-135F tanker high above the Mediterranean during another transfer to Chad in 1986. (Jean-Francois Lipka)

Hissene Habré (left) with one of his most important allies, French President Francois Mitterrand. (Albert Grandolini Collection)

Time and again, some of the newly-arrived C.160NG Transalls were reconfigured to serve as tankers. Here, one of them is about to provide fuel to a Mirage F.1C from EC.5. (Jean-Francois Lipka)

The crew of this 20mm flak protecting Abéche airfield is watching as an AdA Transall transport passes by after landing. (Albert Grandolini Collection)

A TELAR of the Crotale SAM site protecting N'Djamena seen against the backdrop of one of the recently upgraded C-135FR tankers (powered by modern CFM56-2B1 turbofans in place of the older Pratt & Whitney J57s). (Albert Grandolini Collection)

Above: Because of the relatively small size of the military side of N'Djamena IAP, and that airport's vulnerability to Libyan air strikes, the AdA tended to keep only the absolute minimum of its combat aircraft based there. Time and again during Operation Épervier, additional aircraft were deployed, resulting in a tarmac chock full of Jaguars from EC.3 and EC.11: no less than nine of these can be seen in this photograph. (Albert Grandolini Collection)

Left: A Mirage F.1CR (code 33-TB) escorting an Atlantic (serial 15) over the Sahara Desert in central Chad. (Albert Grandolini Collection)

Below: A Mirage F.1C from EC.5 armed with Matra Super 530F (installed underwing, under a white shroud), and wing-tip-mounted Matra R.550 Magic Mk.1 air-to-air missiles (AAM), on alert at N'Djamena IAP. (Albert Grandolini Collection)

Overall, thanks to a host of reorganizations, upgrades and acquisitions motivated by earlier experiences, the French military developed a very strong expeditionary capability, the kind of which turned into a prototype for similar forces developed by most other major Western military powers in the 1990s.

Collapse of the GUNT

The string of GUNT and Libyan defeats in February and March 1986 resulted in the Libyans being massively discredited in the eyes of their Chadian allies, and deep rifts developing within Oueddei's organization. Attempting to distract from the worsening situation, the GUNT attempted an attack from Salal on Moussoro on 20 May. However, this was detected – rather by accident – by the AdA's Centaure radar, while still well away, and quickly beaten back. On the next day, a LAAF MiG-23 approached the area, as recalled by Sergeant Bourdil:

> When the radar contact approached to about 32 kilometres [20 miles] we called our MANPAD team to prepare for air defences. At 16 kilometres [10 miles] out, I put the team on alert and granted them permission to open fire. Then I heard on the radio, 'visual': the MANPAD team reported a 'Jaguar' at about 11 kilometres distance [7 miles] turning north and climbing. It was actually a MiG-23BN that took a look at us. When I looked at my radar display, I could see it disappearing in [a northerly] direction at Mach 1.2. ... The next day, a MiG-25 appeared at high altitude and Mach 0.7. A pair of Mirage F.1CRs and an Atlantic were in the area too, but flying very low. I decided to attempt vectoring Mirages to intercept, but that was not a lot of fun ... after a few minutes, [the] pilots announced 'unable', meaning they reached the maximum altitude and could not go any higher. At that point, the enemy turned left and distanced northbound. [The] Mirages cut his turn and called, 'visual, MiG-25'. Number two locked-on his radar on the MiG. This was jammed by the Libyan, but he locked-on again. Everything was ready, but we did not receive permission to open fire from HQ in N'Djamena.

In absence of success in war, the morale within the GUNT collapsed. Eventually, Oueddei's vice-president, Kamougue, resigned and took with him nearly 2,000 combatants from southern Chad in August 1986. A few minor factions followed in similar fashion, but the major blow came in September, when thousands of Tobou tribesmen

of the People's Armed Forces (Forces Armées Poulaires, FAP) – the largest component of the GUNT – defected and fled into the mountains of Tibesti Massif. Oueddei was thus left with only about 2,000 Arab combatants of the Democratic Revolutionary Council (Conseil Démocratique Révolutionnaire, CDR; also known as the New Vulcan Army), led by Acheikh Ibn Oumar. Worse was soon to follow, as Oueddei then also clashed with Gaddafi: on 10 October, he was injured and arrested during a shoot-out in Tripoli. After recovering from his injuries, he was exiled to Algeria.

This de-facto collapse of the GUNT was a particularly severe blow for the Libyan military in Chad, which was designed to provide combat and logistical support for its Chadian allies. Without the Chadians, the Libyans had not only lost their major reconnaissance and assault infantry force, but they found themselves confronted by an increasingly hostile local population and their supply lines were exposed to hit-and-run attacks by the FAP. While well fortified and armed, the major Libyan bases in Wadi Doum, Faya Largeau, Fada, Bardai, Zouar and Yebbi Bou were all isolated and had to be resupplied by transport aircraft.

The Libyans deployed a 2,500-strong force commanded by Colonel Ar-Rifi and whatever was left of the GUNT to search for and destroy the FAP in Tibesti. In some cases, they attempted to pursue defecting columns towards the south. This development was carefully monitored by the AdA, which was running a series of 'armed-reconnaissance' missions over northern Chad at the time, code-named 'Operation Fennec'. At an unknown date in mid-November, a pair of Jaguars escorted by a Mirage F.1C came across a GUNT column of two AML-90s and eight trucks between Ennedi and Erdi, and destroyed it completely with 200 30mm cannon shells and 38 68mm unguided rockets.[65]

Later the same month, the FAP in Tibesti found itself cut off

The Transall transports of different AdA units – but also those assigned to the secretive GAM.56 – became extremely active in late 1986, when they were not only hauling supplies for forward-deployed FANT units, but also para-dropped fuel and ammunition for FAP insurgents that defected from the GUNT in northern Chad. This example was filmed while braking hard on a very uneven surface of a forward landing strip in the Kalait area. (Tom Cooper Collection)

from supplies. Habré quickly seized the opportunity: instead of alienating the Chadians that were distanced from the GUNT and Gaddafi, he established contacts with them. After two FANT convoys loaded with supplies failed to reach Tibesti, he requested Paris to help. From 8 December, Transalls assigned to one of the most secretive units of the AdA, the Mixed Aerial Group 56 (Groupe Aérien Mixte, GAM.56 'Vaucluse'), began flying nocturnal resupply missions for the FAP in the Zouar area.[66] Usually, two aircraft flew such missions by night, their crews using US-supplied night-vision goggles (NVGs) to operate at very low altitudes before delivering their load with the help of parachutes. Another such mission is known to have been flown to the Zouar area on 16 December.[67]

Fuel and ammunition enabled the FAP to continue launching attacks on enemy supply convoys, but in turn provoked a vicious Libyan reaction. After several days of sustained air strikes by the LAAF (during which insurgents claimed one 'Libyan MiG' as shot down), several Libyan columns converged on Bardai, Zouar and Wour and captured all three places. Immediately afterwards, the LAAF began flying air strikes on the FAP in Ounianga Kebir while its Mi-25s began providing top cover for all movements of ground forces, including supply convoys.

Battle of Fada

Despite the fierce Libyan reaction, the FAP proved successful in keeping the Libyans preoccupied in northern Chad in late 1986. In turn, this bought time for Habré's Commander-in-Chief, Hassan Djamous, to complete preparations for a large operation to liberate the country. By December 1986, Djamous managed to assemble two major groups of FANT at Kalait and Ziguei, where two big supply depots were established. These were well-supplied with the help of Chadian, but also US and French transports.[68]

Once ready, and with French troops and combat aircraft providing protection for southern Chad, Djamous launched a probing attack north of the Red Line. A column with about 3,000 FANT combatants moved out of Kalait on 31 December 1986 and quickly overran the Libyan garrison of Zouar. Exploiting this success, and using their intricate knowledge of the local terrain, Chadians then quickly advanced on Fada, garrisoned by about 1,000 Libyan troops and between 300 and 400 CDR militia. Using classic desert nomad tactics of mounted attacks, the FANT assaulted on the evening of 2 January 1987, taking their enemy completely by surprise. Several outposts about 40km south of Fada were overrun within less than an hour, before the main force raced at high speed over minefields directly at the town. One part of the force then attacked the headquarters while the other turned around to attack the Libyan defenders from the rear. Attempting to counter Toyotas that were racing around them, Libyan infantry fought mounted in BMP-1s, supported by T-55s: but both types proved unable to turn their turrets rapidly enough to track the attacking Chadians and were death traps for their crews. They were easily overcome and knocked out in droves, usually by RPG-7 hits at point-blank range. Shocked by the ferocity of the

Two out of a total of 13 Libyan T-55s knocked out during the Battle of Fada. Both show traces of strikes by Milan ATGMs.
(Albert Grandolini Collection)

A Libyan P-15 'Flat Face' radar captured during the Battle of Fada in early January 1987. (Albert Grandolini Collection)

FANT onslaught, surviving Libyans attempted to withdraw and regroup at the local airfield, but were almost annihilated in the brutal battle. While their commander – Colonel al-Mabouq – and about 50 officers managed to escape on board an Antonov An-26 transport aircraft, 784 troops left behind were killed. They lost 92 T-55 MBTs and 33 BMP-1 IFVs destroyed, with six SIAI-Marchetti SF.260 light-strikers, one Mi-25 helicopter gunship, 13 T-55s, 118 BMP-1s, one P-15 radar (ASCC-code 'Flat Face') and 81 soldiers captured. Achieving all this, the FANT lost only 18 troops killed in action (KIA) and three Toyotas destroyed. The Battle of Fada thus ended in the first major defeat of the Libyan military in Chad.[69]

As much as it was shocking, the rout at Fada prompted Gaddafi into action. The LAAF received orders to fly strikes against all insurgent and FANT-held towns and villages north of the Red Line. Tu-22s bombed Fada and Zouar on 3 January, followed by Su-22s. Meanwhile, Libyan ground forces in Chad were reinforced to around 11,000 troops and ordered to recapture Fada. When reports about air strikes and troop deployments reached N'Djamena, Habré reacted by requesting help from the French air force. However, fearing a possible escalation, Paris only agreed to bolster its troop presence to 2,500, and furnish additional military aid worth FF250 million, including 10 launchers and 250 Milan ATGMs, 15 TRC-40 long-range radios, trucks and 12 more AML-90 armoured cars. Nevertheless, it seems that the 11e Choc did receive permission to support the FANT advance, because the LAAF is known to have suffered several losses during the following days, including a Mi-25 shot down on 4 January and a MiG-23 on 5 January, both while attacking Fada.[70] Only when the Libyans then began deploying Tu-22 bombers to strike Oum Chalouba and Arada, south of the Red Line, on 4 January, did the government in Paris see such actions as an open provocation. Certainly, the French were then repeatedly crossing the Red Line too: for example, AdA Transalls were involved in hauling supplies to the FANT force and evacuating casualties and captured Libyans from Fada (one of them picked up a ZRK-BD 9K31 Strela-1 [ASCC-code SA-9 Gaskin] SAM-system captured intact).[71] Now, with the tide clearly in favour of Habré's FANT, the French decided to increase pressure on the Libyans by curtailing LAAF activity over the battlefield. Late on 5 January, the AdA HQ at N'Djamena IAP received an order from Paris to raid the LAAF early warning radar site at Wadi Doum.

Martel Riders

French fighter-bombers and reconnaissance fighters were active over eastern Chad during January 1987. Commandant Yvon Goutx, CO of the ER.33 detachment at N'Djamena IAP, recalled:

> Our first mission was to monitor the Sudanese border and track possible deployment of reinforcements for Oueddei from that direction, on 31 December. We flew two additional sorties on 1 and 2 January. By 3 January, the situation became critical enough for us to receive the order to switch to air defence mission: Libyans had crossed the Red Line and bombed Oum Chalouba and Arada; [a] few bombs even fell near French Army positions in [the] Kalait area. ... [The] AdA had Mirage F.1C interceptors of EC.3/12 deployed at N'Djamena, but their navigation system was rather rudimentary. It required support from [a] ground-based radar network. In France, that was no problem, but in Chad we had nothing but [a] few surveillance radars and systems associated with HAWK and Crotale SAM sites deployed to protect N'Djamena and Moussoro. That's why we had to accompany them with Jaguars or Mirage F.1CRs.
>
> Together with Lieutenant Plasse I flew one reconnaissance sortie in a Mirage F.1CR that was configured with two external tanks of 1,200 litres, two Matra R.550 Magic Mk.1 missiles,

a Barax jammer, a Phimat pod, and a launcher for 18 decoy cartridges installed instead of [a] braking parachute. Plasse's Mirage carried a ventral tank, two Magics, one Matra Super 530, and [the] same ECM-pods as mine. We were eager to find and shoot down a MiG or one of [the] Il-76 transports, but all our efforts were frustrated by [the] Libyans.[72]

Organizing a new strike on Wadi Doum proved harder than expected because – concerned about the possibility of another Libyan air strike on N'Djamena IAP – the AdA had meanwhile scattered most of its aircraft to airfields in neighbouring countries. Therefore, the decision was taken for four Jaguar As from EC.3/3 Ardennes deployed at Bangui IAP in the Central African Republic to fly this mission, each armed with one AS.37 Martel ADAM anti-radar missile.[73]

Targeting intelligence for the mission was much more precise than during the first French attack on this airfield, flown in February 1986 (see Part 2 for details), and the pilots were informed about the presence of one SA-6 SAM site and eight ZSU-23-4 vehicles in the target zone.

The second raid on Wadi Doum was launched in the early morning of 6 January – and it began badly: Guy Wurtz, one of the Jaguar pilots, detected a failure of his Martel missile during the final pre-flight check and was forced to abort. The other three pilots – Jean-Paul Saussier, Patrick Guy and Thierry Lebourg – still launched. They rendezvoused with a C-135F tanker escorted by two Mirage F.1Cs from EC.3/12 south of the Red Line and topped up their fuel tanks before proceeding further north. However, on approaching the target zone, the pilots were informed by the crew of an Atlantic MPA that only the Libyan early warning radar in Faya Largeau was active. The mission was therefore aborted and all three Jaguars returned to N'Djamena IAP with their Martels still on board.[74] Later the same day, additional Jaguars and Mirage F.1Cs followed them to the airport of the Chadian capital, increasing the total number of AdA aircraft deployed there to 26. During the evening, AdA commanders and pilots set up a conference to discuss their options. Commandant André Carbon, a veteran of the first raid on Wadi Doum, recalled:

> There were two options: [an] anti-radar attack on Wadi Doum or [an] attack on Aouzou airfield [Tanoua AB; authors' note]. We preferred the anti-radar option, but this necessitated [the] Libyans to activate their radars. Eventually, we found a way to make them do that.

Like the Mirage F.1C interceptors of the AdA, most Libyan aircraft required ground control support for safe navigation over the expanses of the Sahara. Ground control depended on radars to do its job. With their intelligence indicating that Tanoua and Ma'arten as-Sahra air bases would be bristling with activity on the next day, the French concluded that the Libyans would activate most of their radars. One Atlantic MPA was launched at 0800 on 7 January and sent north to detect Libyan radar emissions over northern Chad. Meanwhile, ground crews armed four Jaguars

A rare photograph showing two EC.3 Jaguar As after their landing at N'Djamena IAP, following the unsuccessful first anti-radar strike on Wadi Doum on 6 January 1987. Each aircraft is carrying a single AS.37 Martel anti-radar missile under the centreline. (SIRPA-AIR)

with Martels, while eight others were prepared for an attack on Tanoua. Carbon continued:

> I was to lead eight Jaguars armed with rocket launchers for [an] attack on Aouzou, if that option [was] exercised. We spent the morning waiting for [the] signal from Atlantic that 'tickled' the 16th Parallel in expectation of Libyans switching on their radars. … It was almost 0920 but Atlantic still hadn't detect[ed] anything. The C-135F tanker then called to announce that it had no fuel to deliver to two escorting Mirage F.1Cs left. Without top cover, the slow MPA would have to abort its mission and return to N'Djamena. [The] commander of our mission, Lieutenant-Colonel Peccavy, was on board and he asked them for one more pass. It was his birthday so the crew agreed: it was during that last pass, around 0930, that the Flat Face at Wadi Doum started emitting.[75]

The French compound at N'Djamena IAP exploded into activity. Following another quick briefing and final checks, crews mounted their aircraft and then rolled for take-off. The first to launch, at 1100, were Mirage F.1CRs flown by Yvon Goutx and Claude Dishly. They were followed by four Jaguars armed with Martels and four Mirage F.1Cs that were to provide top cover.[76]

All three formations met with tankers that orbited south of the Red Line, roughly between Ati and Abéche, and topped up their fuel tanks. While other C-135Fs then turned south, one continued north with the Jaguars for an additional 290km (180 miles), to help them adjust their nav/attack systems.

Meanwhile, Goutx and Dishly proceeded towards a position north-west of Faya Largeau at an altitude of only 91 metres (300ft) and speed of 400km/h (248mph) – well below the horizon of Libyan early warning radars. Around 1250, they entered a climb to 1,828m (6,000ft) and then turned to a course of 90 degrees – straight towards Wadi Doum. Technicians on board the Atlantic registered a near-instant Libyan reaction: a P-19 at Wadi Doum was activated, followed by a number of other radars, all of which began emitting at full power in order to better track two French fighters that seemingly appeared 'out of nowhere' deep within LAAF-controlled airspace.[77]

The Jaguar A serial A100/11-MP suffered a technical malfunction of its Martel missile during the first anti-radar attack on Wadi Doum on 6 January 1987, which was cancelled after the involved Atlantic found no suitable Libyan emissions. After its missile was quickly repaired at N'Djamena IAP, it participated in the second – and much more successful – raid on Wadi Doum AB a day later. (Albert Grandolini Collection)

The successful pair of the second anti-radar raid on Wadi Doum AB: a Jaguar A (code 11-MP, foreground) with an Atlantic (serial 27) in flight over eastern Chad. (Albert Grandolini Collection)

Unknown to the Libyans, by that time four Jaguars armed with Martels were only 111km (68 miles) south of Wadi Doum: flying at less than 60m (200ft) above the ground and a speed of 926km/h (500knots), they remained undetected until it was too late. Goutx continued:

> Thierry Lebourg and Guy Wurtz were in front, about two kilometres from each other and ahead of the other pair. At about 64km (39 miles) from Wadi Doum they climbed to 91m (300ft), and acquired their target. It was exactly 1300 when Guy fired his missile at the Flat Face. The second pair, Jean-Paul Saussier and Patrick Guy, followed up behind them, but

The temporary camouflage pattern of this Jaguar from EC.11/4 was showing clear traces of very heavy wear after a nearly year-long deployment in Chad (gauging by its frame that remained un-camouflaged, even the cockpit hood was replaced by the time this photograph was taken). Unsurprisingly, the AdA experienced some maintenance problems with the type and aborts occurred from time to time. (Albert Grandolini)

The 1S91 SURN fire-control system ('Straight Flush') of the Libyan SA-6 SAM site at Wadi Doum after its capture by the FANT on 2021 March 1987. (Albert Grandolini Collection)

they could not lock-on on the 'Straight Flush' fire-control radar of the SA-6 SAM site.

After firing one Martel, all the Jaguars descended back to 60m and turned south. Meanwhile, the two Mirage F.1CRs continued approaching Wadi Doum, but descended to less than 152m (500ft). About 20km (12.4miles) from Wadi Doum, Dishly was locked-on by a fire-control radar – probably from one of the Libyan ZSU-23-4s: this prompted both pilots to descend to less than 33m (100ft) and accelerate to 1055km/h (570 knots) in a southerly direction: with their task of acting as a decoy for the Libyans completed, the two Mirages disengaged.

All AdA aircraft involved in the attack returned safely to N'Djamena. It was only during the de-briefing that the crew of the Atlantic informed Dishly that he was pursued by one of the LAAF MiG-23 interceptors around the same time his aircraft was locked-on by the ZSU-23-4. The MiG followed the Mirages into their turn and then pursued them for nearly 100km before turning away because it was short of fuel.

Overall, this second attack on Wadi Doum was declared a success by the French, who – using ELINT/SIGINT reconnaissance only – assessed that the sole AS.37 Martel had knocked out a Libyan P-19 early warning radar. The only available Libyan source informed about this affair does not deny the French success but insists that the radar that was actually knocked out was the 1S91

SURN fire-control system (i.e. Straight Flush radar) of one of their SA-6 SAM sites that were protecting Wadi Doum.[78]

Catastrophe at Wadi Doum

Following the fall of Fada, Gaddafi ordered the mobilization of all reservists and deployment of additional reinforcements to Chad. This was accomplished primarily by transport aircraft of the LAAF, which hauled ever more troops and supplies to Faya Largeau and Wadi Doum. Through February, Libyan Army strength in the country increased to about 14,500 troops, supported by hundreds of tanks, IFVs and heavy artillery. Over 4,000 troops were concentrated in the Wadi Doum area alone, where an elaborate system of all-round and in-depth defences which were considered impregnable was constructed to protect the air base that sometimes accommodated up to 20 LAAF aircraft and helicopters on a temporary basis. The latter saw intensive activity against any FANT columns detected while raiding the areas north of Faya Largeau. For example, on 10 February, SF.260s fired rockets at a number of vehicles of a FANT column north-west of Fada. Subsequently, the effectiveness of these began to drop due to the presence of Chadian teams armed with FIM-43A Red Eye and SA-7 MANPADs: these claimed a Mirage 5D shot down over the Oum Chalouba area in early January, at least one Mi-25 near Zouar on 19 February and a SF.260 near Fada on 14 March.[79]

Hit by up to 50 Libyan air strikes a day, the FAP then redirected its efforts to the Zouar area, again distracting Libyan attention from developments further south, where the FANT and AdA were busy hauling reinforcements to Fada in preparation for a renewed advance: waging a mobile war in the expanses of the Sahara required immense stockpiles of water, food, and ammunition, most of which had to be flown in from N'Djamena. The Chadians took some time to plan their next step. Ahead of them were two major Libyan strongpoints in northern Chad, Faya Largeau in the west and, slightly closer to Fada, Wadi Doum. Following extensive studies, they concluded that they could ignore the former: should the FANT manage to reduce the heavily protected Wadi Doum before continuing further north, the position of any Libyans in Faya Largeau would become untenable.

Libyan forces made the next move: in early March, two of their mechanized battalions moved out of Wadi Doum in the direction of Fada. The SIGINT element of the 11e Choc detected this advance and the FANT reacted by deploying several of its companies to shadow the enemy while concentrating about 2,400 troops for a counter-attack. On 19 March, at 0700, Chadians – reinforced by the Stinger- team of the 11e Choc, French forward air controllers (FACs), and a team of the US Marine Corps that was operating several Pioneer unmanned aerial vehicles (UAVs) – ambushed the southernmost column near Bir Koran, about 50km south-east of Wadi Doum: after a volley of Milan ATGMs knocked out several T-55s, the Chadians swarmed forward and overran the Libyans, killing 384 and capturing 47. Either Chadian Red Eyes or Stingers also shot down an LAAF SF.260. The next morning, the FANT repeated the exercise against the second Libyan column: this time killing 467, capturing 89 and downing an LAAF Mi-8.[80]

As the surviving Libyans fell back to the north, Hassan Djamous decided to launch a pursuit. At the time, he was not authorized to attack Wadi Doum and his force was actually considered too weak for this task: but the opportunity of inflicting heavy losses on a retreating enemy was too good to ignore. His decision proved correct: with FANT Toyotas and AML-90s on their heels, the Libyans fled to Wadi Doum, revealing gaps in minefields and showing their pursuers the way while spreading panic among the defenders. Replenished with ammunition and fuel delivered to the front by French Army Aérospatiale SA.330B Puma helicopters, Djamous ordered his force to attack. He was grievously injured shortly after as his vehicle hit a mine while approaching the southern perimeter of Wadi Doum and had to be evacuated by one of the Pumas. Nevertheless, the attack continued without him with the FANT first assaulting the rocky plateau that housed an early warning radar site, including several P-15 and P-19 radars. Quickly overcoming Libyan resistance, heedless of risk, the Toyotas then drove down the slope right into the air base: the control tower was destroyed by several Milan missiles, causing the Libyans to panic. One of the LAAF flight controllers at Wadi Doum described the scenes of chaos and panic:

> We were permanently on duty, with only short breaks in between. On 21 March 1987, I was awakened by [the] sound of detonations. ... I ordered one aircraft to get airborne and let us know where the enemy [was]. The pilot took off amid great confusion, with enemy shells falling around him. Other pilots then scrambled to take off in haste – abandoning us. I attempted to contact the base commander on the radio. After many attempts, an unknown voice replied, 'You son of a bitch!' Then I understood that the commander had surely been killed. I left the tower and found refuge within the [reinforced] Operations Command Post, where I also found the officer in charge of air defences.[81]

The only aircraft that actually managed to get away was one of the LAAF C-130Hs: it took off pursued by several Milan ATGMs. A Mi-25 and a SF.260 that attempted to scramble immediately afterwards were both shot down. From that moment on, it was everybody for himself as the Libyans proved unable to offer any kind of coordinated defence, letting the Chadians maraud around the base, drive behind entrenched tanks and knock them out with RPG-7s, recoilless rifles or even hand-grenades thrown into the hatches.

By the time the FANT troops had finally run out of steam, Wadi Doum had become a synonym for Libya's military catastrophe in Chad: 1,269 Libyan Army troops were KIA, and 438 – including their zone commander, Colonel Khalifa Haftar – captured (Haftar's deputy, Colonel Gassim Ali Abou Naour, was killed during the assault on the command post). The list of equipment that was destroyed or captured was huge. The Libyans lost 89 MBTs (including 42 T-55s and 12 T-62s captured), 120 BMP-1 IFVs destroyed or captured, more than 400 other vehicles

Burned-out hulks of Libyan T-55s littered the length and breadth of the battlefield after the fighting for Wadi Doum AB. (via Pit Weinert)

This T-55 was captured intact after its crew abandoned it next to the 3,800-metres long runway of Wadi Doum AB. The vehicle was camouflaged in wide stripes of sand colour, applied roughly over its original olive green finish. (Albert Grandolini Collection)

Another ace up the FANT's sleeve during the fighting in northern Chad in 1987 were Panhard VTT armoured cars armed with launchers for HOT ATGMs, two of which are seen on this photograph. (Albert Grandolini Collection)

As well as Toyota 4WDs, the FANT made heavy use of Panhrad VTT armoured cars, equipped with 20mm automatic cannons, during the battle at Wadi Doum. (Albert Grandolini Collection)

A Libyan P-12 (ASCC-code 'Spoon Rest') radar station, captured on the low hill south of Wadi Doum AB, which was overrun by the FANT quite early during the battle. (Albert Grandolini Collection)

The fin of one of two LAAF An-26s destroyed at Wadi Doum AB – serial number 8213. (Albert Grandolini Collection)

Wreckage of an SF.260 (foreground), two L-39s (left) and another SF.260 destroyed by the FANT at Wadi Doum AB. Wreckage of another SF.260 – serial number 434 – was found nearby, semi-buried in sand. (via Pit Weinert)

destroyed or captured, 12 BM-21s, 11 Aero L-39 Albatros jet trainers (seven were captured intact), 12 SF.260s (five captured intact), two An-26 transports, four Mi-25s (one intact), five Mi-8s, two intact SA-6 SAM sites, two ZSU-23-4s and immense supplies of fuel, water and ammunition.[82]

Although not obvious at the time, the loss of Wadi Doum sealed the fate of Libyan ambitions in Chad. The catastrophe not only

prompted their remaining allies to rally to Habré's side, but also made the Libyan position in Faya Largeau untenable – exactly as predicted by Djamous. As soon as the FANT moved only a few of its companies in that direction, the garrison gave up: using a sandstorm as cover, 2,500 Libyans withdrew north in a long column. Faya Largeau was thus liberated without any fighting on 27 March, followed by Ounianga Kebir three days later.[83]

Petty Bickering

The amount of modern, Soviet-made military equipment captured intact at Fada, Wadi Doum and Faya Largeau raised plenty of interest all over the world – and caused some disagreement over its distribution between Chadians and their allies. Habré certainly had a hand in the affair, as he was attempting to play off Americans against the French in order to obtain more military aid. However, he always preferred his old allies in Paris and could ill-avoid disappointing them because of his overdependence on French support. Therefore, the P-15 radar and two of the seven SA-7 MANPADs captured in Fada were quickly donated to Paris and flown out with help of AdA Transalls.

By early April 1987, at least 27 French military specialists were deployed by Puma helicopters to Wadi Doum to inspect and sort out all the captured equipment. Fierce Libyan air strikes forced their temporary withdrawal, but the FANT took care to disperse and camouflage the most precious booty. On 14 April, an AdA Douglas DC-8 transport brought a team of US military specialists – including five civilians – to N'Djamena. However, the DGSE prevented them from embarking a Chadian C-130A for a flight to Wadi Doum and it is unclear if they were permitted to continue their voyage later on.

Eventually, the affair caused such tension that Habré – concerned about the immense popularity of his successful commanders – began accusing the DGSE of bribing his men and plotting coups against him. He specifically demanded the withdrawal of the 11e Choc from Chad, in turn prompting French Defence Minister Andre Giraud to bluntly threaten to stop all military cooperation with Chad. A solution was found through the French – apparently with some help from Israel and/or the USA – making some of the captured SAMs operational and training Chadians in their use. Libyan air strikes on Wadi Doum were said to have stopped only once a French-operated SA-6 SAM site shot down a MiG-25RB reconnaissance-bomber in late April.[84]

This LAAF Mi-25 (serial number 302) was captured intact by the FANT at Wadi Doum AB. (US Army)

As soon as Libyan air strikes ceased, the Americans launched Operation Mount Hope III with the aim of extracting captured L-39s. This task was accomplished by a team of technicians deployed to Wadi Doum by a USAF C-130 on 6 May. They dismantled all seven jets and loaded them on to the Hercules for transport to N'Djamena, one by one, every day the following week.

The removal of captured radars and SAMs proved much more complex, and an agreement was reached only in September whereby the Americans and French were allocated the same amount of SA-6s (two TELs and three missiles each) and SA-13s (one TEL and one missile each). Because the French had already received the P-15 captured at Fada, the Americans were given the P-19 taken at Wadi Doum. All of this equipment was flown out by USAF Lockheed C-5A Galaxy transports; SAMs and radars destined for France were delivered straight to the AdA's Test Centre (Centre d'Expérience Aérienne Militaire, CEAM) at Mont de Marsan.[85]

The final extraction operation involved two captured Mi-25s. The one at Wadi Doum was taken over by the Americans – in exchange for paying US$2 million to the FANT and delivering a batch of FIM-92A Stingers – and brought out with help of a US Army Boeing CH-47 Chinook helicopter, while the French took away the Mi-25 captured at Fada. Both were eventually flown out of Chad by C-5As – together with three BMP-1 IFVs.

On 21 May 1988, the US Army launched Operation Mount Hope III with the intention of picking up the captured Mi-25. After preparations lasting nearly a month, a giant Lockheed C-5A Galaxy transport of the USAF deployed one CH-47 helicopter of the 160th Special Operations Aviation Group (Airborne) – or SOAG-A – from Fort Campbell (Kentucky) to N'Djamena. The 160th SOAG-A's Chinook is shown hauling the partially disassembled Mi-25 away from Wadi Doum AB. (US Army)

On 21 June 1988, the captured Mi-25 finally arrived at N'Djamena IAP, where it was loaded into a C-5A (seen here) and flown to the USA. (US Army)

After the Chadians donated the intact Libyan Mi-25 serial number 302 to the Americans, the French were left with no choice but to pick up the other captured Mi-25 – serial number 297 – which was actually shot down by the FANT during the Battle of Fada. The helicopter was disassembled and brought to N'Djamena, from where it was flown to France by a USAF C-5A. (8e RPIMA Collection)

Distribution of Libyan SA-13s captured by the FANT caused some dispute between Chadians, the French and Americans. Eventually, all were evenly distributed between the allies. (Albert Grandolini)

An Oasis on Fire

The fall of Wadi Doum and Faya Largeau not only caused another shock in Tripoli, but an outright outcry from Moscow, which demanded that the Libyans destroy as much of their abandoned equipment as possible. The LAAF reacted with an all-out effort against the FANT in northern Chad. Deploying about 70 combat aircraft – including Mirages, Sukhois, L-39s, SF.260s, Tu-22 bombers, but also Il-76 transports that disgorged bombs out of their rear loading ramp – it heavily bombed Wadi Doum AB several times a day for the following weeks. Each airstrike was preceded by a pair of MiG-25PDSs that flew a combat air patrol over the target area in order to remove any possible French interceptors. How much damage the air strikes actually caused remains unknown: not only did it take days for the Chadians, French and Americans to find, count and secure all the equipment captured, but neither Libyans nor Chadians ever published a reliable accounts of LAAF air strikes during this period of the war. While Chadian and French sources usually insist that most of the bombs missed, they do admit that FANT troops sometimes panicked because of air attacks. Whatever happened, it is certain that Habré personally and repeatedly demanded that his Western allies train his troops in the use of some of the heavy SAMs captured from the Libyans, that LAAF air strikes against Wadi Doum stopped in late April and that Chadian MANPAD teams saw plenty of action during March. The latter are known to have claimed a Mirage shot down in the Zouar area on 28 March, an SF.260 further north a day later and a MiG-23BN over Wadi Doum on 7 April.[86]

The subsequent pace of operations decreased as both sides prepared for further fighting. The Libyans scrambled to heavily fortify the Aouzou strip and expand their air base in Ma'arten as-Sahra oasis, in southern Libya, while Habré and his commanders were keen to continue their offensive into northern Chad. The US administration of President Reagan proved very enthusiastic about such ideas: it not only encouraged further military preparations but also promised additional military aid worth US$25 million – in addition to US$16 million already budgeted for 1988.

However, out of fear that Gaddafi might be provoked to fight an all-out war, the French did their best to dissuade Habré from continuing the advance.[87] When the Chadians showed little interest in negotiations, the government in Paris went as far as to suspend deliveries of some of the promised military aid and scale down the size of its military contingent deployed in the country to less than 1,700.[88] With Tripoli signalling no intention of abandoning the Aouzou strip but only expressing the wish to buy back all of its lost equipment, Habré protested and the French were left with no choice but to support military operations against the Libyans around Tibesti and Aouzou.

Eventually, Paris not only deployed a de-mining team into Habré's hometown, Faya Largeau, but also permitted AdA C.160s to haul supplies and troops to new FANT bases in the north, and then extended its assistance to maintenance of all of the FANT's heavy equipment, including AML-90s. Furthermore, the AdT redeployed several of its units north of the 16th Parallel, while the AdA started work on extending the airfield in Abéche with the aim of enabling Mirage F.1Cs to operate from there. When operating from Abéche, AdA interceptors could patrol over north-eastern Chad without the aid of tanker aircraft. Similarly, Mirage F.1CRs were capable of tracking Libyan troop movements inside western Sudan, which were ongoing all through early 1987.[89]

Another reason for the French decision to support a FANT advance into northern Chad was the continuation of the LAAF's bombing campaign through April and May. This threat became obvious when Habré decided to celebrate the Chadian National Day (or 'Liberation Day') in Faya Largeau, his recently liberated hometown, on 7 June. The AdA provided top cover for this occasion in the form of combat air patrols flown by pairs of Mirage

A massive explosion caused by FAB-1500 bombs released by LAAF Tu-22s that attempted to destroy some of the equipment abandoned at Wadi Doum AB. In the foreground are three captured BMP-1s. (Albert Grandolini Collection)

The pilot of a LAAF MiG-25P with his mount armed with two R-40 air-to-air missiles. Libyan MiG-25s regularly escorted air strikes flown by LAAF Tu-22s and Il-76s against major forward bases of the FANT in northern Chad in 1987. (via Pit Weinert)

F.1Cs. Before long, a Libyan Il-76 approached from the north: this was quickly intercepted by the French, who fired several warnings shots across its nose, forcing the Libyans to hurriedly leave the area.[90]

Four Aouzou Battles

The battle for the Aouzou strip began in late July, with the FANT advancing into north-western Chad with the aim of securing its western flank before attacking in the centre. The Libyans reacted with a massive counteroffensive, in the course of which several columns totalling about 3,000 troops attempted to capture Tibesti Massif. When one of these drove in the direction of Bardai, on the morning of 8 August, it was ambushed by a 400-strong FANT force at Oumchi, a water-place about 80km south of Aouzou village, and largely destroyed. Once again, the surviving Libyans fell back in panic, fleeing all the way back to Aouzou – with the FANT on their heels. This pursuit stopped only when the Chadians drew into the village of Aouzou and quickly defeated the local garrison later the same day. Between there and Oumchi, the Libyans had left a long trail of 111 military vehicles destroyed or captured, and 650 troops KIA: 147 were taken prisoner.

The LAAF reacted quickly, deploying more than 70 aircraft

in a vicious bombardment of Aouzou, Wour, Bardai, Zour, and Ounianga Kebir. While causing very little damage to local FANT bases, these air strikes killed dozens of civilians and caused unrest in N'Djamena. On orders from Paris, AdA Mirage F.1Cs flew CAPs along the 16th Parallel, but their pilots were denied permission to operate against Libyans further north. Instead of ordering an interception of Libyan bombers, Paris only protested over LAAF air strikes on villages south of the Red Line.

Libyan military intelligence knew that the FANT advance on Aouzou was heavily supported by the French. Although AdA Mirage F.1Cs were only flying CAPs along the 16th Parallel and were never permitted to operate further north, French Transalls were heavily involved in hauling additional ammunition – including 52 Milan ATGMs and 400 90mm shells taken directly from the AdT's stocks – to bases in northern Chad. Two groups of French troops were present at Faya Largeau oasis, including a detachment from the 17th Parachute Engineer Regiment (Régiment de Génie Parachutiste, 17e RGP) responsible for de-mining operations, and a detachment training Chadians to use captured SA-13s. Therefore, the LAAF was ordered to also bomb Faya Largeau on the morning of 9 August. The strike was flown by one Tu-22 escorted by the usual pair of MiG-25s, with the bomber making two runs, dropping five 500kg bombs each time. One string of the bombs hit an ammunition depot, causing a huge conflagration that killed dozens of FANT troops and civilians, while another destroyed a French military truck parked at the local airport.

Faya was bombed again on 11 August, but this time in a different fashion, as recalled by Patrice Rombaut, who served with the 17e RGP at that time:

[F]irst we saw a flight of two MiG-25s, which I immediately recognized because I was passionate about fighter jets. A day earlier, we were warned about a possible air strike and each section was assigned a shelter for such cases. By then we knew that [the] appearance of a pair of MiG-25s meant that an attack by [a] Tu-22 was imminent. Around 06.00hrs in the morning [sic], we were put on alert and then saw an Il-76 approaching us at an altitude of 5,000 metres (16,404ft), to drop several pallets loaded with bombs.

The Chadians, who were by now left with only a few FIM-43As and captured SA-7s, could clearly not defend themselves against such attacks. Therefore, a Stinger-equipped team from the 11th Marine Artillery Regiment (Régiment d'Artillerie de Marine, 11e RAMa) was deployed to bolster air defences at Faya the next day. The French did not operate in that area alone, however: on 20 August, they shot down a LAAF Mirage over Bardai.[91] Otherwise, their presence was insufficient to deter the Libyans: on 25 August, an Il-76 released eight bombs, while five days later two Il-76s released a total of 24 bombs over Faya Largeau, causing additional casualties to the local population.

Meanwhile, the Libyan military unleashed its full might against

A Libyan Mi-8, shot down by the FANT during the fighting for the Aouzou strip. (Albert Grandolini Collection)

The pilot of this L-39, named Hadi Yusuf Asabaa (front cockpit), narrowly escaped death after his jet received several hits from small-arms fire. (Vaclav Havner Collection)

about 400 FANT troops who entrenched themselves in Aouzou village. A brigade of Jamhuriya Guard led by Colonel Ali ash-Sharif launched its first counter-attack there on 14 August, but this was repulsed. On 19 August, the second assault began with heavy air strikes from Tanoua AB, only 50km away. These caused lots of damage, including the destruction of eight AML-90s, four VLRA technicals with 20mm cannons and six Milan launchers, although the Chadians claimed to have shot down six MiG-23s, one Su-22s, two Mi-8s and one Mi-25 in return.[92] Eventually, the Jamhuriya Guard launched a set-piece assault supported by tremendous volumes of fire-power that forced the surviving Chadians out of Auozou on 28 August. On the following morning, the place was secured by Libyan Army commandos deployed by CH-47 Chinook helicopters.

Raid on Ma'arten as-Sahra

Simultaneously with counter-attacking at Aouzou, a brigade-sized Libyan force moved in the direction of Ounianga Kebir. During the first clash with the FANT in this area, on 24 and 25 August, the Chadians shot down a LAAF Mirage 5D and a MiG-23BN, the pilots of both of which were captured. The Mirage pilot was Libyan Captain Abdel Majid Salofara, while the MiG was flown by Lieutenant Colonel Mohammed Mahmoud al-Qam, a Palestinian. This was just the start of the final Libyan catastrophe in this war. On 5 September, the Libyan brigade was outflanked by several FANT battalions and smashed a few kilometres outside Ounianga Kebir.

On the same day, Hassan Djamous – who had barely recovered from his injuries – led a raiding force of 2,000 across the Libyan border and well to the east of the battlefield, before turning west and assaulting Ma'arten as-Sahra. Taking about 3,000 defenders – including a well-equipped Libyan Army brigade – completely by surprise, the FANT attacked the place for hours, killing more than 1,700 Libyans, destroying about 70 MBTs, 30 IFVs, at least one SAM and one radar site, knocking out and blowing up whatever they could not carry away, and shooting down two Mi-25s. The local air base was completely demolished, together with 26 aircraft and helicopters – including several MiG-21s, three MiG-23s, four Mirage F.1s and a few Su-22s – and 312 officers, pilots, technicians and other personnel were taken prisoner. While the Chadians continued demolishing Libyan facilities during the following night, four AdA C.160s and two AAT C-130As flew out all the captives straight to N'Djamena. By dawn on 6 September, the FANT – which suffered a loss of 65 killed and 112 wounded during this operation – loaded as much loot as possible into their vehicles and disappeared in a southerly direction.[93]

Last Cry of the Blinder

If defeats at Fada and Wadi Doum shocked him, the raid on Ma'arten sa-Sahra left Gaddafi stunned. Stubborn as always, instead of realizing that the war in Chad was lost, he ordered an all-out attack, including new air strikes by Tu-22s, the deployment of chemical weapons, and a large-scale ground offensive to recover Aouzou. French intelligence received reports of these moves, and thus all the AdA, AdT, DGSE and FANT units were put on alert on the morning 7 September. At 0400, two Mirage F.1Cs (call-sign Condor Whisky, flown by lieutenants Delannoy and Brill) were scrambled to fly a CAP over N'Djamena, followed by two others (call-sign Condor X-Ray), an Atlantic MPA and a C-135F tanker, shortly later. The Hawk SAM site was also put on alert.

Around 0655, the Centaure radar station at N'Djamena IAP detected an unknown aircraft approaching at high speed over Nigerian airspace to about 88.5km (55 miles) and not responding to IFF Mode 1 nor Mode 3 interrogations. Condor-Whisky was vectored to intercept, but while approaching their target, both Mirage pilots reported difficulties in attempting to achieve a radar lock-on: instead of one, their radar displays showed two targets

A LAAF Tu-22 bomber high above the Mediterranean in early 1977. Ten years later, these supersonic bombers still looked very much the same, except that the pan-Arabic tri-colore in red-white-black was replaced by green roundels. (USN)

at bearing 215, 45km (28 miles) away, with one at an altitude of 5,486m (18,000ft) and the other at 3,657m (12,000ft). When it became clear that the radars of both Mirages were jammed, they were ordered to turn away and keep their distance, while the task of intercepting the target was forwarded to the 403eme RA's HAWK SAM site.

The incoming aircraft was a LAAF Tu-22 bomber flying along a carefully selected route: an international airline corridor over Niger, Nigeria and Cameroon. As soon as the fire-control radar of the French SAM site locked on to it, the big Tupolev descended to 4,000m (13,123ft) and accelerated to 1,000km/h (540 knots). By that time, the TACAN emitter and Centaure radar at N'Djamena were turned off, while the French activated a fake AN/TPS decoy radar emitter in case of the Libyans attempting to deploy anti-radar missiles. Two minutes later, the Centaure radar was switched on again and the AN/TPS decoy turned off: all of a sudden, the French realized that the Tu-22 was only 13km (8 miles) away and entering Chadian airspace. The first firing unit of the MIM-23B I-HAWK site then turned into high-power illumination mode, and received orders to open fire – but nothing happened: a technical malfunction swung the launcher in the wrong direction. The crew quickly changed to the second firing unit and this finally fired one HAWK: a few seconds later, the missile scored a direct hit, striking the rear fuselage of the bomber as it flew through thin cloud cover, about 1,000m (3,280ft) above the ground, with an open bomb bay and aligning with the runway of N'Djamena IAP. A powerful detonation ripped the Tu-22 into three large parts that crashed in flames, hitting the ground only a few hundred metres outside Camp Dubut of the French Army. The crew of three was instantly killed.[94]

News of the successful interception of a Libyan Tu-22 over N'Djamena barely reached Abéche when another Tu-22 approached the airfield, around 0720. The AdA Crotale site was already on alert, but the Centaure radar supporting it experienced a malfunction the previous day, significantly degrading the low-altitude detection capability of the French SAM site. This snag was reported to N'Djamena by radio and it is likely that the Libyans were also aware of this problem: the Tu-22 took the French by surprise by approaching at low altitude and using the cover of surrounding hills before starting a bombing run with the sun at its back.

The bomber was detected by the French when only 15km (9 miles) away, thundering at 888km/h at an altitude of 457m

One of 12 launchers of the 403e RA's MIM-23B I-HAWK SAM site in position outside N'Djamena IAP but covered by tarpaulin for protection from the sun. (Albert Grandolini Collection)

When the Tu-22 was hit, its four 1,500kg FAB-1500 bombs were not yet armed. Therefore, all four impacted the ground without detonating. This FAB-1500 was recovered by troops of the 403e RA and put on display outside their HQ. (Albert Grandolini Collection)

(1,500ft) directly along the runway axis – all set for a perfect bombing run. The Crotale site went into action, and detected and tracked the incoming Libyan Tu-22 with its TV-system: the order to open fire was issued as the bomber was near the minimum engagement range!

The SAM site fired two missiles: the first followed an erratic course before self-destructing, while the second began pursuing

The undercarriage of the Libyan Tu-22 shot down near N'Djamena on 7 September 1987 was used as the background for a memorial to the 403e RA's success. (Albert Grandolini Collection)

We were about to land, when ground control advised me to listen to the frequency used by the radar in N'Djamena and a pair of Mirages. I could hear the Mirage leader calling, 'Full throttle, drop tanks away! Radar contact … visual on an Il-76.' The ground control asked, 'confirm, Il-76?' The reply was, 'Affirmative'. Then, 'Order for destruction!' … The leader locked-on, folded the guard cap over his trigger and was about to open fire, when his wingman called, 'Leader, Stop! … I think the aircraft is a C-141 StarLifter!' Uncertain, the two pilots approached their target and confirmed, 'visual on C-141 … US Air Force … serial number 40638!' Meanwhile, our flight turned around in [the] direction of Bangui, but we kept on listening as the Mirages forced the Americans to land at N'Djamena. The aircraft was impounded there for a day, the captain explaining he was returning from some diplomatic mission and failed to read NOTAMs [notices filed for pilots warning them of hazards along a flight route]. We never knew if that was some sort of a test or error, but there were no further incursions into the no-fly-zone.[97]

the aircraft, prompting the navigator of the Tu-22 to open fire at the missile with its 23mm tail-gun and start ejecting chaff and flares. The Crotale exploded harmlessly behind its target, but evasive manoeuvring resulted in the four FAB-1500 missing the runway. By that time, a third missile was airborne and pursuing the departing bomber: it also failed to hit, as did a fourth missile, fired from a range of 2,500m (2,734 yards) as the Tu-22 was already accelerating away. The French were very lucky, as the four massive bombs released by the Tupolev caused only some slight damage to one of the newly built hangars. Abéche airfield remained operational and four Mirage F.1Cs were deployed there to bolster its defences.[95]

The C-141 Incident

These two raids and the downing of a LAAF Tu-22 over N'Djamena brought the situation to the verge of spiralling out of control. On 8 September, Libyan An-26 transports dropped bombs filled with the Yperit-B chemical weapon on several FANT positions over Chad.[96] Reports of this spread rapidly throughout Chad and the French military forces deployed in the country. However, despite Habré's persistent demands for retaliation strikes on Libya, the government in Paris rushed to de-escalate situation and began exercising severe pressure upon both belligerents to stop the war. Eventually, president of Chad and the Libyan leader accepted and a ceasefire was agreed, starting on 11 September.

Tensions, however, remained high among AdA Mirage crews who were still limited to flying CAPs along the Red Line. On 9 September, an unidentified aircraft was detected while transiting the 'no-fly zone' between the Red Line and N'Djamena, and two Mirage F.1Cs vectored to intercept. The leader of the French pair identified his target as an 'Il-76' – identical to LAAF transports that frequently bombed Faya Largeau. He locked on his radar and prepared to open fire. Commandant Pierre-Alain Antoine was flying with a flight of Jaguar As from EC.3/3 that were in the process of transferring from Bangui to N'Djamena when the drama took place:

Libyan Il-76s were, however, active over northern Chad the next day, right around the time a team from the 403eme RA was in the process of searching for a suitable position in Faya Largeau area for redeployment of its MIM-23B I-HAWK SAM site. Habré insisted that Faya receive its traditional administrative and political role, and demanded that the French not only extend and strengthen the airfield there but also provide necessary air defences. Already alarmed by reports of the Libyan deployment of chemical weapons, all French personnel rapidly sought nearby bomb shelters as soon as the air raid alert was sounded, around 1600. As usual, a Tu-22 appeared high in the sky – apparently escorted by at least one MiG-25. After circling the target, the bomber made a perfect approach out of the sun and dropped 10 500kg FAB-500M54 bombs. A Stinger team from the 11e RAMa and Chadian SA-7s returned fire, but in vain: their missiles were decoyed by flares deployed by the Libyan bomber or self-destructed at the limit of their trajectory. Bombs thus literally rained down on the oasis, striking another Chadian ammunition depot and narrowly missing the AdT's Camp Goumiers. Once again, most of casualties were local civilians: the injured were flown out by Chadian C-130s and French C.160s. Also flown out was the team of the 403eme RA: after this experience, local authorities found their presence 'undesirable'.

Byzantine Negotiations

After the ceasefire, and despite severe pressure from the USA on N'Djamena to continue the conflict until toppling Gaddafi, the Chadian, French and Libyan governments intensified their efforts to find a peaceful solution. Probably due of feeling more isolated on the international scene, the Libyan leader declared himself ready to normalize relations and recognize Habré as the legitimate president of Chad. As subsequent developments were to show, although forced to give up his expansionist project towards Chad, Gaddafi was actually only buying time to find a different solution.

Tensions along the border between Chad and Libya remained high for many months and the situation was characterized by countless breaches of the ceasefire, which continued for the next three years. Some of these breaches were caused by impulsive and unproductive outbursts of anger by the Libyans; others were related to Chadian refusals to exchange prisoners of war – an aspect that became ever more important for Gaddafi, who found himself facing a defeated, disillusioned and angry armed forces and public at home. Furthermore, Libyan military intelligence quickly discovered that some of their military personnel held in Chad were recruited by the Central Intelligence Agency (CIA), with the intention of creating an armed opposition group.[98]

The LAAF remained very active over northern Chad for most of the second half of 1987, flying reconnaissance over Zouar, Bardai, Gouro, Yebbi Bou, Zoumri and even Abéche, south of the 16th Parallel. In other cases, it attacked FANT units in the Aouzou area. Colonel Ali Thani, by then a seasoned veteran with several tours of duty in Chad, recalled his last mission flown on a MiG-23BN, on 8 October 1987:

> [A] Su-22 flown by Captain Dia ad-Din was shot down by a MANPAD in [the] Aouzou area and I flew top cover for the Mi-8 underway to recover him. I found ad-Din's crash site and flew an orbit overhead, but then my aircraft was hit too. I ejected and was recovered by the Mi-8; ad-Din was captured by Chadian troops.[99]

The French military did not react to any of the Libyan incursions – often infuriating the Chadians. Instead, the AdA only promised to accelerate the work on Abéche airfield in order to make it capable of supporting Mirage F.1-operations. President Mitterrand even sent his personal military advisor to Habré, to warn him that should Chadian forces cross the Libyan border again, Paris would cancel all military support for Chad. The Chadian president reacted with warnings that the FANT had used nearly 90 percent of the supplies provided so far and was critically short on ammunition. Furthermore, up to 60 percent of its vehicles were either lost in combat or out of service and in need of repair. He concluded that the Libyan military proved much more active and efficient in defending its own soil: according to him, the FANT lost 18 AML-90s knocked out by the LAAF and 15 by Libyan-fired Milan ATGMs during August and September 1987.[100]

Mitterrand, however, remained insistent. A reconstructed airfield in Abéche received its first Mirage F.1s in November 1987, but otherwise the AdA was only granted to fly 100 hours a month in support of the FANT in northern Chad: most of the authorized effort was spent in using C.160s to supply Chadian garrisons in the Tibesti and Aouzou areas. This decision hit the FANT quite hard, because around that time the French also withdrew most of their military personnel who used to serve with the AAT, which then also lost the services of one of its four C-130As (the aircraft in question, registered as TT-PAB, caught fire after landing at an airstrip near Yebbi Bou). Another Chadian Hercules was meanwhile in need of repairs and stranded at N'Djamena IAP, while the remaining two examples (registrations TT-PAD and TT-PAE) were undergoing overhauls in Portugal and France.

Refusing to be drawn into the conflict again, Mitterrand then authorized the DGSE to make use of aircraft of Minerve and Sfair airlines – including several Lockheed L-100s (civilian variant of the C-130 Hercules), operated by French civilian personnel recruited by private companies.

Nevertheless, motivated by their own designs against Gaddafi, the Americans were more than pleased to continue providing aid to Habré. As well as delivering the above-mentioned batch of Stingers and paying US$2 million for one of the captured Libyan Mi-25s, Washington granted aid worth US$15.4 million to secure overhauls of all the remaining C-130s and the acquisition of new supplies and arms. Furthermore, Iraq delivered military equipment and ammunition worth US$2 million on board four Il-76 transports in early 1988, while about 100 FANT officers and NCOS were sent to Iraq for training. Finally, even China deployed a team of about 30 military technicians to Chad in late 1988: they helped overhaul a number of captured Libyan T-55s.

During the summer of 1988, there were indications that the Libyans – growing impatient over lack of success in negotiations – might launch a new offensive into Chad. LAAF Mirage 5DRs and MiG-25Rs flew a series of reconnaissance sorties over Bardai, Ounianga Kebir and Faya Largeau on 7 and 8 July.[101] By that time, three Stinger-equipped teams of the 35th Airborne Artillery Regiment (Régiment Artillerie Aéroportées, 35e RAP) of the AdT were deployed in the Faya Largeau area. One of them recalled an incident that remains a mystery to this day:

> We had three Stinger teams arranged in three positions around the Rock of Mao – a hill we used for quick friend or foe identification. Any friendly aircraft had to arrive facing the rock, turn on the landing lights, fly at a specific altitude etc. Around 20:00 on 7 July 1988, an unidentified aircraft approached Faya Largeau at an altitude of about 400 or 500 metres. It made a pass without respecting identification criteria, with its rear cargo door open and alight, leaving plenty of vapour in its trail. Chemical alert was sounded and everybody donned his full NBC kit, while gunners received permission to open fire. During its second pass, the aircraft – identified as 'C-130' – switched on its headlight. When it was about 3 or 4 kilometres away, all three teams fired their Stingers. The first developed a technical problem, the second self-destructed after reaching the end of its trajectory, but the third hit the target and detonated. The area where this aircraft should have crashed to the ground was prohibited for us because it was heavily mined. The next morning an Atlantic circled around there for about 15 minutes and then disappeared. Some gunners from the 35e RAP were then quickly pulled out and replaced by others, for unknown reasons, and without anybody ever letting us know what was shot down.[102]

One of two LAAF Tu-22s abandoned at Mitiga AB, shown in the early 2000s. (via Pit Weinert)

Libyan troops with a cache of arms captured from the FANT – including several grip-stocks for US-made FIM-43A Red Eye MANPADs.
(Albert Grandolini Collection)

The operational days of this ex-USAF C-130A ended when the aircraft caught fire and was abandoned at Yebbi Bou in late 1987.
(Albert Grandolini Collection)

It remains unknown what the gunners of the 35e RAP hit that evening. One possibility is that it was a LAAF An-26, but at least as likely it was a friendly transport – perhaps one of the Lockheed L-100s known to have been chartered by various US intelligence agencies for their own purposes – or even a civilian aircraft.

Meanwhile, the Libyan Army reorganized the 'Islamic Legion' – a unit consisting of foreign mercenaries that was its primary tool during operations in Chad in the early 1980s – into the 'Green Legion'. Staffed by about 3,200 Palestinians, 2,400 Yemenis and hundreds of Lebanese, this was deployed to reinforce garrisons in Sebha, Ma'arten as-Sahra, Aouzou and elsewhere along the border with Chad. Gaddafi also sponsored the revival of Oueddei's armed force – the 'Neo-GUNT': through alliances with various local insurgent groups, this grew to about 8,000 combatants in August 1988.[103] The LAAF was also reinforced, through the arrival of a group of 173 pilots and ground personnel from Syria. Two new hardened runways were constructed near Toumo, while Ma'arten as-Sahra AB was reconstructed and reopened in September 1988, to house a squadron each of SF.260s and L-39s. Alarmed by such developments, France pushed for another series of negotiations. Finally, Chad and Libya re-established diplomatic relations in October 1988, in turn agreeing to hold a summit between Gaddafi and Habré at Bamako, in Mali, in July 1989. During this tense meeting and rather Byzantine negotiations, the two leaders agreed to sign a peace accord in Algiers on 31 August of the same year.[104]

Despite the eventual success of negotiations, the Libyans subsequently infiltrated about 3,000 Neo-GUNT troops into Sudan, from where they began launching attacks on the FANT in Chad – often supported by LAAF SF.260s. One of the latter was shot down over Omm on 28 November 1988, and its crew – 1st Lieutenant Ali Saleh and Sergeant Mohammed Mahdi – was captured. The Neo-GUNT was only neutralized in 1989, primarily through Iraq-sponsored negotiations that caused nearly 2,000 of its combatants to defect.[105] By that time, Habré was at odds with most FANT commanders. Although his power rested on that of his military, the Chadian president proved unwilling to introduce necessary reforms. When his commanders began opposing him, Habré ordered their assassination: Djamous was murdered in April 1989 but Idris Deby escaped to Sudan, where he found plenty of followers among the local Zaghawas. With Libyan support, and due to the French refusal to continue propping up Habré, Deby launched an invasion of Chad in October 1990 and forced Habré into exile, taking over on 10 November of that year. Twenty-six years later, he is still in charge of a French-supported government in N'Djamena.[106]

CHAPTER 5
FINAL CLASH

Because of the flow of developments and the involvement of various political leaders and different Western intelligence agencies, many details about the Chadian Wars of the 1970s and 1980s remain unknown today – including casualty figures for all involved parties. This is unlikely to change any time soon.

Although deeply shocked by the US strikes in April 1986, and then repeatedly rocked by severe defeats in Chad, and despite becoming much less vocal in his support for international terrorism, Muammar el-Gaddafi remained one of main backers for many militant groups around the world for several years to come. While moderating his public rhetoric, he began acting with discernible restraint and thus it often took years for Western governments to find evidence of direct links between Tripoli and a series of anti-US actions between 1987 and 1990. Not only the USA, but the entire Western world changed its strategy in dealing with Libya, from one of open military action to covert activities in support of Libyan opposition and legal prosecution of the country and its leaders.

This was especially so after two bombings of airliners in the late 1980s. On 21 December 1988, a bomb exploded in the cargo hold of the Pan Am's Boeing 747-121A (registration N739PA) operated on Flight 103, causing it to crash into the Scottish town of Lockerbie, killing all 244 passengers and 15 crew on board, plus 11 people on the ground. Less than a year later, on 19 September 1989, a mid-air explosion ripped apart the McDonnell Douglas DC-10-30 (registration N54629) of the French airline UTA (Union de Transports Aériens) on Flight 772, flying from N'Djamena to Paris, killing 170 occupants.

In both cases, early suspicions fell on various groups without links to Libya. When it came to Flight 103, the USA suspected the Syrian-based Popular Front for the Liberation of Palestine – General Command (PFLP-GC) or the government of the Islamic Republic of Iran as revenge for the US Navy shooting down an IranAir airliner over the Persian Gulf in July 1988. In the case of Flight 772, the French suspected the Palestinian Islamic Jihad or the Secret Chadian Resistance. However, on 14 November 1991, the USA and Scotland indicted two Libyan intelligence officials for their roles in the bombing of Flight 103 with the help of Swiss timing devices supplied to Libya. Similarly, on 10 March 1999, a French court found six Libyans guilty in absentia of bombing the UTA's DC-10.[107]

Instead of launching a punitive military action, both superpowers acted through international diplomacy and the courts. Eventually, the United Nations Security Council (UNSC) passed three resolutions concerning the Pan Am 103 and UTA 772 bombings. Resolution 731 of 21 January 1992 called upon Libya to extradite the two accused bombers. Resolution 748 of 31 March 1992 imposed significant sanctions on Libya – including mandatory

Locals inspecting pieces of wreckage of the UTA's DC-10, which was bombed while flying from N'Djamena to Paris on 19 September 1989. (Albert Grandolini Collection)

economic sanctions, a ban on all civilian air links and an arms embargo – until Libya turned over the two suspects to British or US authorities for trial. Resolution 883 of 11 November 1993 banned sales of oil equipment to Libya and placed a limited freeze on Libyan foreign assets. Over a decade later, all of these actions resulted in Tripoli eventually paying billions in compensation to victims and their families in these two and 24 other terrorist attacks.

Surprisingly, similar steps were also taken in regards of another issue between the USA and Libya, which at a certain point in the late 1980s appeared to have resulted in the final military confrontation between Washington and Tripoli of the decade.

A Factory in Rabta

Libyan efforts to obtain weapons of mass destruction were primarily motivated by the drive to compensate for the country's military weaknesses relative to its likely opponents – mainly Israel, but also Egypt and the USA.

Although Libya signed the Nuclear Non-proliferation Treaty in 1975, it was around the same time that Gaddafi repeatedly went on record to stress that the Arabs need a nuclear weapons capability to match Israel's, and that he attempted to buy nuclear weapons from China. Over the following years, Libya then tried to reach a deal for nuclear weapons with India in 1978, and negotiated nuclear technology sharing arrangements with Pakistan in 1980, the Soviet Union in 1981, Argentina in 1983, Brazil in 1984 and Belgium in 1985.[108] However, all such efforts proved overambitious and only resulted in the Soviets constructing a small research reactor. Instead, Gaddafi embarked on his own chemical weapons (CW) programme in the 1980s as a much more cost-effective way of bolstering his military might.

Over time, three factories were built: the first one, designated 'Pharma-150', was constructed at Rabta, about 120km (70

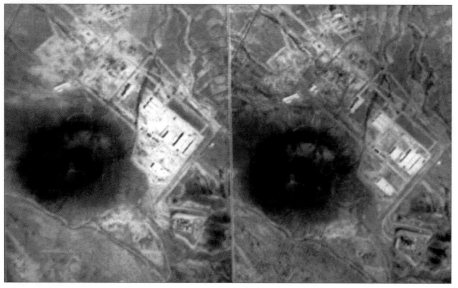

Two satellite images (made by the French 'Spot' satellite) of the Pharma-150, or Rabta, factory in 1990. (Albert Grandolini Collection)

A still from a video showing the front of the Rabta factory in 1988. (Albert Grandolini Collection)

The End of the LAAF's Development

Whether by accident or design, bans and embargoes resulting from the bombings of Flights 103 and 772, and the Libyan CW-programme, also had direct repercussions for the further development of the LAAF. Most notable among these was the cancellation of a Libyan project to replace their problematic Tu-22s with at least 36 Sukhoi Su-24MK fighter-bombers. Out of an initial order for 12 such aircraft, only six were delivered in 1989, when they entered service with the newly established No. 1024 Squadron. Similar projects for the upgrade of all of MiG-23MLs to MiG-23MLD-standard, and the replacement of the remaining MiG-21s and MiG-23s with MiG-29s were never realized. Instead, and following repeated dissatisfaction with lack of cooperation with Moscow, the LAAF began sending its MiG-23s for overhaul in Bulgria during the late 1970s.

Furthermore, after evacuating most of its aircraft from Benina AB, the LAAF decided to keep its units dispersed. Benina remained a main terminal for delivery and assembly of MiG-23s – for example following their overhauls abroad – and it retained the main maintenance facility for all variants of this type. However, the MiG-23MF/MS-equipped No. 1050 Squadron and MiG-23BN-equipped No. 1070 Squadron moved to al-Bumbah AB, north-west of Tobruk, while an unknown unit equipped with MiG-23BNs and the MiG-23MF/MS-equipped No. 1060 Squadron moved to al-Abraq AB, near Derna. For similar reasons, the Su-22s of No. 1032 Squadron were re-deployed to Woutia AB, in western Libya, near the Tunisian border. These rearrangements – some of which were prompted by Gaddafi's increased suspicion of his officers, especially in the wake of a wave of dissatisfaction that spread through the country after defeat in Chad – ultimately prevented the planned introduction of the wing-structure within the LAAF.

Another project that was cancelled was related to a potentially significant effort to improve the range of LAAF MiG-23s. In 1987, the Libyan government contracted the West German company Intec Technical Trade und Logistic GmbH (ITTL) to develop and adapt IFR probes on different types of combat aircraft in Libyan service. Initially using IFR probes obtained from France to modify one MiG-23BN and one MiG-23UB from No. 1070 Squadron, ITTL then went a step further and developed IFR probes of indigenous design, which were installed on another MiG-23BN. Simultaneously, the West Germans converted

miles) south of Tripoli; the second, named 'Pharma-200', was constructed underground at the Sebha army base; and the third, 'Pharma-300' or 'Rabta II', was at Tarhuna. Initial reports about work on the factories emerged in the early 1980s, and such allegations exacerbated international suspicion of Libya over the following years. After the Libyans deployed CW bombs during the final days of the Chadian War, Western analysts became concerned about Gaddafi's willingness and capacity to employ such weapons elsewhere. In 1988, President Reagan publicly announced the possibility of a military strike on the Rabta plant, prompting a Gaddafi denial, asserting instead that the plant was used for the manufacture of pharmaceuticals and that his government accepted international controls banning the use of chemical weapons. By that time, it was known that the West German company Imhausen-Chemie had been contracted by Tripoli for work on the Rabta plant in April 1980, and that over time a total of 12 firms from Western and Eastern Europe became involved in the project.[109] Keen to keep CWs out of Libya, Reagan applied pressure on West Germany to halt the export of related technology, materials and expertise.

one of the LAAF's C-130s to serve as a tanker aircraft through installing a refuelling system into the cargo hold and indigenous IFR pods on underwing pylons. Flight testing of the resulting KC-130H tanker showed that while Libyan Mirage F.1AD pilots experienced no major problems, their MiG-23 colleagues could

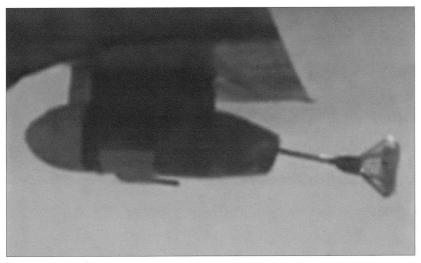

A still from a video showing the IFR pod developed by ITTL and installed on the outboard underwing pylon of one of the LAAF C-130Hs. (Tom Cooper Collection)

Another still from the same video showing the 'basket' being released from the ITTL's pod. (Tom Cooper Collection)

Sometime in 1988, the pilot of this Mirage F.1AD made the first successful contact with the IFR basket made by the ITTL, proving the validity of the West German design. (Tom Cooper Collection)

barely control their aircraft at the rather slow cruising speed of the converted Hercules, which was only about 400km/h (215 knots). The decision was taken to install the same pods on LAAF Il-76s. The resulting conversion work, and flight testing including one Il-76 and two Mirage F.1Ads, was barely completed by the time that public uproar over the involvement of West German companies in support of Gaddafi resulted in the cancellation of all of related projects.[110] Another of the catalysts for this negative outcome was the final incident between US Navy fighters and the Libyan Arab Air Force in the 1980s.

Chemical Reaction

As tensions between the USA and Libya continued to rise, the US 6th Fleet's CVBG around USS *John F. Kennedy* (CV-67) departed Cannes in France on 1 January 1989, setting a course for the central Mediterranean. Sailing in the direction of the port of Haifa in Israel, not in any relation to the dispute over Libyan CW projects, the aircraft of CVW-3 embarked on board the *Kennedy* ran a series of routine exercises in the airspace between the Greek island of Crete and the northern Libyan coast.

On 4 January, a group of A-6Es from VA-75 was exercising south of Crete, about 130km north of Libya, escorted by two pairs of F-14As from VF-32 and an E-2C from VAW-126, in what the USN calls 'non-provocative, day cyclic operations'. The southernmost CAP station was occupied by Tomcats flown by Commander Joseph B. Connelly, with Commander Leo F. Enwright in the back seat (flying the F-14A modex AC207, BuAerNo 159610), and Lieutenant Hermon C. Cook III, with Lieutenant Commander Steven Patrick Collins (flying the F-14A modex AC202, BuAerNo 159437). Due to heightened tensions with Libya, both crews were specially briefed for this mission and took off somewhat in a rush, their aircraft armed with four AIM-7 Sparrows but only two instead of the usual four AIM-9 Sidewinders.[111]

At 1150, the E-2C informed the Tomcat crews about the launch of two MiG-23MFs of No. 1050 Squadron, LAAF, from al-Bumbah AB, north-west of Tobruq. The F-14s turned in a south-easterly direction and acquired the Libyans with their AWG-9 radars as they were 115km (72 miles) away, immediately recognizing them as a pair. The MiGs initially moved north-east, then east. After tracking them with their radars for a few seconds, both Tomcats turned south-west – away from the Libyans but the latter then reacted with a sharp, 90 degrees turn in a northerly direction, thus initiating an engagement. Unknown to the

During the latter stage of its work in Libya, the ITTL adapted two of its pods on one of the LAAF's Il-76 transports (coded 5A-DNP). Test runs, including two Mirage F.1ADs, proved successful.
(Tom Cooper Collection)

Table 2: Composition of CVW-3 (USS *John F. Kennedy*), early 1989

Aircraft Carrier	Carrier Air Wing & Squadrons	Aircraft Type & Modex	Duration of Deployment & Notes
USS *John F. Kennedy* (CV-67)	CVW-3	(AC)	25 August 1985 – 16 April 1986
	VF-14 Tophatters	F-14A AC100	
	VF-32 Swordsmen	F-14A AC200	
	VA-46 Clansmen	A-7E AC300	
	VA-72 Blue Hawks	A-7E AC400	
	VA-75 Sunday Punchers	A-6E/KA-6D AC500	
	VAW-126 Seahawks	E-2C AC600	
	HS-7 Big Dippers	SH-3H AC610	
	VAQ-130 Zappers	EA-6B AC620	
	VS-22 Vidars	S-3A AC700	

LAAF, the USN had introduced an entirely new set of Rules of Engagement (ROEs) for such situations off the coast of Libya. Based on their experiences from March 1986 and the fact that the LAAF had meanwhile been equipped with such interceptor types as MiG-23MFs, MiG-23MLs and MiG-25P/PDSs, equipped with medium range air-to-air missiles, the Americans granted permission for their pilots to consider themselves threatened by Libyans even if these did not open fire, but were approaching in a 'threatening fashion'. Between April 1986 and January 1989, nothing of this kind happened: the Libyans meanwhile introduced the practice of turning away from USN F-14s as soon as these would 'paint' them with their radars. This time, it was different.

After the two Libyan MiG-23MFs turned north, they accelerated from 796 to 833km/h (430 to 450 knots) and climbed to 2,743m (9,000ft)), before turning north-west on a new collision-course with the two F-14s. Trying to determine what was going to happen next, the Tomcats turned back south and then south-east, but the Libyans followed each time. As the two formations approached to 56km (35 miles) apart – with the Tomcats meanwhile heading almost directly south and the Libyans directly north, approaching at a combined speed of over 1,852km/h (1,000 knots) – the E-2C

called the F-14-crews to advise them that Libyan intentions were probably hostile and they were free to open fire in self defence even before the MiGs did so. Estimating that the Libyans were armed with Soviet-made R-23 or R-24 medium range air-to-air missiles with an effective range of about 19 kilometres (12 miles), the two Swordsmen crews decided to arm their missiles at a range of about 32 kilometres (20 miles). They also began to gradually descend in order to make themselves more difficult targets for the less sophisticated radars of LAAF MiG-23s.

After trying to turn away from the Libyans for a fifth time, and with the range down to 19km, the two Tomcat crews decided to engage. Enright fired one AIM-7 at the lead MiG, followed by another a few seconds later launched from a range of 16km (10 miles). Both Sparrows appeared to guide at first and streaked towards their target, but as the LAAF pair turned slightly left – in a

Beginning of the end: as of 1989, the LAAF was left with less than 40 operational Mirage 5Ds – aircraft the order of which marked the start of the nearly 20-years long period of massive build-up of the Libyan air power. This photograph is showing the example with serial number 435 – one of at least three that were impounded in France until the March 1990. (Albert Grandolini Collection)

north-westerly direction – both lost the lock-on and missed.

The two F-14s then split, Connelly breaking hard right and Cook hard left, forcing the Libyans to concentrate on one of them: both MiGs turned into Cook, prompting him to reverse his turn and bank left towards his opponents, now about 9.6km (6 miles) away. Not waiting any longer, Cook fired his first Sparrow, head-on, and the missile raced straight for its target, impacting one of the MiG's intakes and causing it to explode in a huge fireball.

As the AC202 turned right to avoid debris from the downed MiG-23, Connelly approached the Libyan wingman from behind. Trying to target it with a Sidewinder, he could not get a good tone alert: after a few frantic seconds, Connelly sorted out the problem with his switches, got a very strong tone and pulled the trigger. The Sidewinder hit the top side of the MiG, causing the pilot to eject.[112]

As they both descended to the safety of a low altitude, both Tomcat crews saw the parachutes of the Libyan pilots and then accelerated north, without waiting for two additional Libyan MiG-23s that had meanwhile been scrambled from al-Bumbah AB.

Exactly why the two MiGs of No. 1050 Squadron were scrambled and then vectored to intercept the two F-14As from VF-32 in this fashion remains unclear to this day. Gaddafi was not only angry enough to call for an emergency session of the United Nations and let his ambassador to the UN accuse the USA of a 'premeditated attack' on two unarmed 'reconnaissance' aircraft: he was also so concerned that he ordered the evacuation of the entire LAAF to air bases in central Libya.[113]

The furore over the shooting-down of the two MiGs and the Rabta factory gradually subdued over the following weeks. Already weakened by his massive defeat in Chad and facing increasing unrest at home, Gaddafi was forced to realize that he could not continue challenging the USA and other Western powers as he had done before. On 20 January 1989, George Bush was inaugurated as the next president of the USA: although he did not signal an immediate improvement in US-Libyan relations, eight years of almost uninterrupted confrontation between the USA and Libya were thus de-facto over. The period of Libyan Air Wars – sometimes characterized by short but sharp, at other times protracted and bitter clashes, thus came to an end: for at least the next 20 years, all further disputes between the four major belligerents of this conflict were negotiated by means of diplomacy and the international courts.

A pair of VF-32 F-14s with a Tomcat modex AC200 (in the background) about a second from launch off one of the two waist catapults of the USS *John F. Kennedy*. (USN)

Modex AC207 was the leading Tomcat of the pair that clashed with Libyan MiG-23MFs on 4 January 1989. This photograph was taken several weeks after that episode. (Tom Cooper Collection)

One of the VF-32 F-14As on the deck of the USS *John F. Kennedy* during the visit to Cannes in late December 1988. (Marc Chiabeau)

The F-14A modex AC202 was flown by the wingman of the VF-32 pair on 4 January 1989: it scored the first kill against one of two Libyan MiG-23MFs. In the background is an F-14A from sister squadron VF-14. (USN)

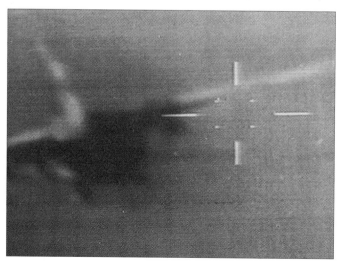

A still from the television-camera-set (TCS) of Connelly's F-14A (AC207), showing the wingman MiG-23MF seconds before this was hit by an AIM-9 Sidewinder. Notable on the MiG are missiles carried on usual hardpoints under each wing and under the fuselage. (USN)

A still from a video showing how the kill marking was originally applied on the F-14A modex AC202. (via Pit Weinert)

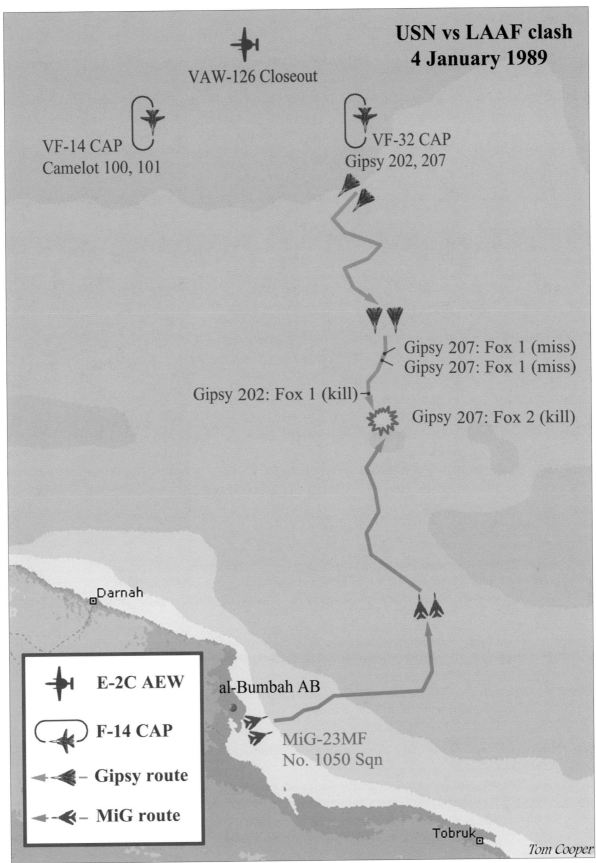

USN vs LAAF clash
4 January 1989

VAW-126 Closeout

VF-14 CAP
Camelot 100, 101

VF-32 CAP
Gipsy 202, 207

Gipsy 207: Fox 1 (miss)
Gipsy 207: Fox 1 (miss)

Gipsy 202: Fox 1 (kill) →

Gipsy 207: Fox 2 (kill)

Darnah

al-Bumbah AB

E-2C AEW

F-14 CAP

Gipsy route

MiG route

MiG-23MF
No. 1050 Sqn

Tobruk

Tom Cooper

A diagram of the air combat between a pair of VF-32 F-14s and a pair of No. 1050 Squadron's MiG-23MFs on 4 January 1989. VF-14's Tomcats used the call-sign 'Camelot', VF-32's 'Gipsy', while the VAW-126 E-2C used the call-sign 'Closeout'.

BIBLIOGRAPHY

Much of the material presented in this book were obtained in the course of research for the book series *Arab MiGs*, which presents the history of Arab air forces at war with Israel. Additional information was acquired during interviews with participants and eyewitnesses mentioned in the Acknowledgments and elsewhere, in Egypt and Libya, but also in France, USA, Iraq and Syria. Sadly, earlier – *very serious and very direct* – threats to the security of specific persons prevented most of them from speaking openly, while the availability of original Libyan documentation remains very limited. Nevertheless, contributions of all people who provided their recollections proved precious and enabled the authors to cross-examine the following publications (as well as those mentioned in footnotes) that were consulted in preparation of this book:

Allam-Mi, A., *Tchad en Guerre: Tractations politiques et diplomatiques, 19751990* (Paris: L'harmattan, 2014).

Armée de l'Air, *Escadron ECT.2/2 Cote d'Or, 1966-1986* (Dijon: AdA, 1986).

Beaumont, H., *Mirage III, Mirage 5, Mirage 50: Toutes les versions en France et dans le Monde* (Clichy Cedex: Larivière, 2005, ISBN 2-84890-079-2).

Bévillard, General A., *La Saga du Transport Aérien Militaire Francais, De Kolwezi à Mazar-e-Sharif, de Port au Prince à Dumont-d'Urville, Tome 1* (Sceaux: l'Esprit du Livre Editions, 2007).

Biedermann, B., Schreyer, H. & Wegmann, B., *Die Militäraufklärung der NVA – Ehemalige Aufklärer berichten: Im Zentrum und im Einsatz (Geheime Nachrichtendienste)* (Berlin: Köster Berlin, 2007, ISBN 978-3895646604).

Blundy, D. & Lycett, A., *Qaddafi and the Libyan Revolution*, (Boston: Little Brown & Co, 1987, ISBN 978-0-316-10042-7).

Brent, W., *African Air Forces* (Nelspruit, S. Africa: Freeworld Publications, 1999).

Chambost, G., *Missions de guerre: Histoires authentiques* (Le Chesnay: Altipresse, 2003, ISBN 978-2911218255).

Chenel, B., Liébert, M. & Moreau, E., *Mirage III/5/50 en service á l'étranger* (Hammeau Les Farges: LELA Presse, 2014).

Collectif, *Chronique du Charles de Gaulle; L'apogée d'un siècle d'aéronautique navale* (Chroniques Them, 2002), ISBN 978-2205053234).

Collectif, *Les avions de Renseignement Electronique, 50 ans d'activités secrètes racontées par les acteurs* (Paris: Lavauzelle/Association Guerrelec, 2009).

Collectif, *Le Jaguar dans ses Missions de Guerre Electronique* (Paris: Lavauzelle/Association Guerrelec, 2007).

Cooper, T., Weinert P., Hinz F. & Lepko M., *African MiGs, MiGs and Sukhois in Service in Sub-Saharan Africa, Volume 1: Angola to Ivory Coast* (Vienna: Harpia Publishing, 2010, ISBN 978-0-9825539-5-4).

Dini, M., 'Istruivo I Libici per conto di Roma', *Europeo Journal*, 28 July 1990.

Drendel, L., *Intruder* (Carrollton: Squadron/Signal Publications Inc., 1991, ISBN 0-89747-263-2).

Ernesto, Fabrizio Di, *Portaerei Italia: Sessant'anni di NATO nel nostro Paese* (Milano: Fuoco Edizioni, 2011).

Faligot, R., Guisnel, J. & Kauffer, R., *Histoire Politique des Services Secrets Français, de la Seconde Guerre Mondiale à nos Jours* (Paris: La Découverte, 2012).

FANT, Glorieuses Victoires des FANT sur l'Armée Libyenne, *Le Heros* No. 8/April 1987 (official magazine of the FANT).

Flintham, V., *Air Wars and Aircraft: a Detailed Record of Air Combat 1945 to the Present* (London: Arms and Armour Press, 1989, ISBN 0-85368-779-X).

Forget, General M., *Nos forces aériennes en Opex, Un demi-siècle d'intervention extérieures* (Paris: Economica, 2013).

Huertas, S.M., *Dassault-Bréguet Mirage III/5* (London: Osprey Publishing, 1990, ISBN 0-85045-933-8).

Irra, M., *The History of the Czechoslovak 1st Fighter Regiment, 19441994* (in Czech), (Ceskych Budejovicich Muzeum, 2014).

Liébert, M. & Buyck, S., *Le Mirage F1 et les Mirage de seconde generation à voilure en fleche, Vol.1: Projets et Prototypes* (Outreau: Éditions Lela Presse, 2007, ISBN 2-914017-40-5).

Liébert, M. & Buyck, S., *Le Mirage F1 et les Mirage de seconde generation à voilure en fleche, Vol.2: Les Mirage F1 desérie, Un avion aux multiples facettes* (Outreau: Éditions Lela Presse, 2014, ISBN 2-914017-41-3).

Lorell, Mark A., *Airpower in Peripheral Conflict: The French Experience in Africa* (Santa Monica: RAND, 1989, ISBN 0-8330-0937-0).

Mantoux, S., *Les guerres du Tchad (1969–1987)*, (Clermont-Ferrand: Lemme edit Illustoria, 2014, ISBN 978-2-917575-49-9).

Martini, F., 'Sigonella 1985 – Cosi fermammo gli USA', *La Repubblica Journal*, 16 April 2003.

Mome Vert, Patrick du, *Mission Oxygène* (Paris: Filipacchi, 1987; ISBN: 978-2850184574).

Nicoli, R., *Cocardi Tricolori Speciale 2: F-104S* (Novara: RN Publishing, 2007).

Nicoli, R., *Corardi Tricolori Speciale 4: F-104G* (Novara: RN Publishing, 2010).

Ougartchinska, R. & Priore, R., *Pour la Peau de Kadhafi: Guerres, Secrets, et Mensonges, 1969–2011* (Paris: Fayard, 2013).

Piccinno, C. & Testa, P.P., 'La strana storia dei pilot di Gheddafi', *Avvenimenti Journal*, 27 July 1993.

Pollack, Kenneth M., *Arabs at War: Military Effectiveness, 1948–1991* (Lincoln, Nebraska: Univesity of Nebraska Press, 2004, ISBN 0-8032-8783-6).

Protti, D. & Provvisionato, S., 'Nemico, ti insegno a uccidere', *Europeo Journal*, 21 July 1990.

Sadik, Brigadier General Ahmad & Cooper, T., *Iraqi Fighters, Camouflage & Markings: 19532003* (Houston: Harpia Publishing LLC, 2008, ISBN 978-0-6152141-4-6).

Sené, F., *Raids Dans le Sahara Central Tchad Libye 1941–1987: Sarra Ou le Rezzou Decisif* (Paris: L'Harmattan, 2011, ISBN 978-2296566446).

Sergievsky, A., 'Fire in the Prairie' (in Russian), *VKO Magazine*, No. 4/17, 2004.

Sharpe, Captain R., *Jane's Fighting Ships 1992–1993* (Coulsdon: Jane's Information Group Ltd., 1992, ISBN 0-7106-0983-3).

Stafrace, C., *Arab Air Forces* (Carolton: Squadron/Signal Publications Inc., 1994, ISBN 0-89747-326-4).

Stafrace, C., *The Air Campaign for the Freedom of Libya, February to October 2011, Operations Odyssey Dawn and Unified Protector (Camouflage & Markings Number 6)*, (Bletchley: Guideline Publications, 2012).

Stanik, Joseph T., *El Dorado Canyon: Reagan's Undeclared War with Qaddafi* (Annapolis: Naval Institute Press, 2002, ISBN 1-55750-983-2).

Storaro, F., *1964–1984: Vent'anni di Aeronautica Militare, Missione Africa/Twenty Years of Italian Air Force, Mission Africa* (Rome: Instituto Bibliografico Napoleone, 2010).

Thoß, B., *Vom Kalten Krieg zur deutschen Einheit* (Oldenburg: Wissenschaftsverlag, 1995, ISBN 978-3486561609).

Turner, J.W., *Continent Ablaze: The Insurgency Wars in Africa 1960 to the Present* (London: Arms & Armour Press, 1998, ISBN 1-85409-128-X).

Valente, D. & Pozzi, P., *Lockheed-Aeritalia F-104 Starfighter* (Milano: Intergest, 1976).

Vezin, Alain, *Jaguar, le félin en action* (Boulogne: ETAI, 2008).

Wegman, B., *Die Militäraufklärung der NVA: Die zentrale Organisation der Militärischen Aufklärung der Streitkräfte der Deutschen Demokratischen Republik* (Berlin: Köster Berlin, 2006, ISBN 978-3895745805).

Willis, D. (ed.), *Aerospace Encyclopaedia of World Air Forces* (London: Aerospace Publishing Ltd., 1999, ISBN 1-86184-045-4).

World Defence Almanac, *Military Technology* magazine volumes 1/91, 1/93, 1/95, 1/97, 1/98 & 1/03.

Zaloga, Steven J., *Red SAM: The SA-2 Guideline Anti-Aircraft Missile* (Oxford: Osprey Publishing Ltd, 2007, ISBN 978-1-84603-062-8).

Zolotaryov, Major General V.A., *Russia in Local Wars and Military Conflicts in the Second Half of the 20th Century* (in Russian), (Moscow: Institute of Military History, Ministry of Defence of the Russian Federation, 2000).

Various volumes of *El-Djeich* Magazine (the official publication of the Algerian Ministry of Defence), *Air Fan, le Fana de l'Aviation, Aviation Magazine Internationale, Air et Cosmos*, and *Raids* (France), *Aviation News* magazine (UK) and personal notes of all the authors based on various other daily and weekly printed publications.

ACKNOWLEDGEMENTS

The authors wish to express their special gratitude to all those individuals who contributed to this book. Foremost of them are several former Libyan Air Force pilots who were forced to leave their country because of issues related to their own safety and that of their family. Some of them have granted interviews only on condition of anonymity, and thus we feel free only to forward our special thanks for providing advice, unique information and insights to Abdoul Hassan, Ali Tani and Hazem al-Bajigni in Libya.

Several retired US Navy pilots and officers have kindly provided advice and interviews too, although – again because of clear, direct and very specific threats for their personal security – they also felt forced to do so on condition of anonymity. The exception we feel free to mention is Dave 'Hey Joe' Parsons, to whom we wish to express our special thanks.

We would also like to forward our expressions of gratitude to a number of veteran French Air Force pilots, servicemen and members of their families, who kindly provided interviews, permission to use their documentation, family archives and photographs, including General Yvon Goutx, Colonel Jean-Pierre Petit, Colonel Pierre-Alain Antoine, Lieutenant-Colonel André Dufour, Commandant André Carbon, Sergeant Thierry Bourdil and Patrice Rombaut.

Other thanks further go to a number of researchers elsewhere, who kindly helped during the work on this book, in particular: Dr David Nicolle in Great Britain, Tom Long in the USA, Arthur Hubers and Jeroen Nijemeijer from the Netherlands, Javier Nat from Spain, Vaclav Havner, Josef Simon and Miroslav Irra from the Czech Republic, Milos Sipos from Slovakia, Pit Weinert from Germany, Marc Chiabeaud from France and Christof Hahn from Austria. All of them provided extensive aid in one or other form of research and eventually made this book possible.

(Endnotes)

1. While theoretically considered equivalent to an NCO rank in USA or Great Britain, the French rank of Aspirant and Major is actually in between officer and NCO ranks, and considered the lowest officer rank, though also the highest NCO rank.

2. Sadik et al., p. 128.

3. Villiers, pp. 197-199.

4. A classic example of a repeat of such reports is Steven J. Zaloga's article 'Tupolev Tu-22 Blinder and Tu-22M Backfire', published in *World Air Power Journal*, Volume 33 (Summer 1998); one of the latest citations in this regard can be found in Franco Storaro's *1964-1984: Twenty Years of Italian Air Force, Mission Africa*, p. 77.

5. Wegmann, p. 285.

6. Thoß, pp. 679-680.

7. Ougartchinska et al., pp. 145-159.

8. Ahmad Allam-Mi, *Tchad en Guerre*, p. 208; the same author reported an additional sortie by a LAAF MiG-25RB in the same area in April 1986, and concluded that such operations might have had their influence upon subsequent decisions of the French government.

9. Stanik, pp. 143-144. Stanik further cites a secret meeting of a US diplomat with Soviet and East German representatives in late March 1986, in the course of which the American apprised the others of the threat emitted by the Libyan 'People's Bureau' – embassy – in East Berlin, for American citizens and property in West Berlin. Demanding the US government produce evidence for allegations against Libya, the Soviets and East Germans refused to take action. Contrary to such findings and the 'official line' of the USA, stand such claims as those of a former agent of the Israeli foreign intelligence service Mossad, Victor Ostrovsky. According to Ostrovsky, the 'irrefutable proof' for Libyan involvement in the bombing of La Belle used by President Reagan was actually fabricated by Mossad. The Israelis convinced their US allies that two Israeli missile boats and a SAAR-4-class corvette approached the coast north of Tripoli and disgorged three groups of special forces operatives who planted so-called 'Trojans' – taps – on selected points in the Libyan telecommunication network, during the night of 17 to 18 February 1986. One of these taps was positioned inside a civilian building just a few blocks outside Bab al-Azizia barracks – Gaddafi's headquarters in the Libyan capital. Actually, so Ostrovsky says, the taps were used by Mossad to mimic a long series of terrorist orders transmitted from Tripoli to various Libyan embassies around the world. The resulting 'Libyan communications' were then quasi-intercepted and provided to the US intelligence agencies, which forwarded them up the chain of command, eventually providing Reagan with 'irrefutable proof' of Libyan involvement. In reality, according to Ostrovsky, the Americans had no clue who bombed La Belle and were facing strong opposition against a military action from the French and Spanish. Supposedly, the governments in Paris and Madrid found it suspicious that several supposedly intercepted Libyan communications were worded similarly to various reports provided to them by Mossad. Furthermore, the Americans could not explain to them how Mossad had no clue who planted the bomb in La Belle. For details, see Ostrovsky, V. & Hoy, C., *By Way of Deception*, (Amer Educational Trust, 1999, ISBN 978-0937165102). While it is certain that charges of Libyans plotting and supporting terrorist activity abounded all over the world in 1985–1986, and that there was no definite proof for most such accusations, some were supported by evidence. As well as the bombing of La Belle – where firm evidence for Libyan involvement was actually obtained only years later conclusive evidence of Libyan involvement was also ascertained for the bombing of a Douglas DC-8 (registration F-BOLL) airliner flying from Brazzaville (in the Democratic Republic of Congo, i.e. Congo-Brazzaville) to Paris, on 10 March 1984. The aircraft made a refuelling stop at N'Djamena IAP when a bomb placed in the cargo compartment detonated, killing one person and injuring 24 others. French intelligence later determined that this bombing was supervised by a Libyan intelligence officer named al-Masri (See Ougartchinska et al., pp.145-159).

10. Serial numbers of some of the reconnaissance aircraft known to have been involved in operations against Libya in the spring of 1986, included: EC-135 & RC-135: 10282, 10285, 12669, 14846, and 14749; SR-71A: 17960, 17980.

11. Stanik, pp.151-152.

12. Robert F. Dorr, 'Operation El Dorado Canyon: Libya Under Air Attack in 1986', *DefenceMediaNetwork*, 7 April 2011. On the contrary, in another interview, one of the mission leaders observed, 'Gaddafi personally wasn't the target … I say that categorically, because it was not the mission's objective.' (see 'How I bombed Qaddafi: a Personal Account of an American Blow Against Terrorism', *Popular Mechanics*, July 1987).

13. Although the USAF had about 30 Lockheed F-117A Night Hawk 'stealth' bombers in service at the time, this type was deleted from selection at an unclear point in time: it was still considered 'top secret' and revealed to the public only two years later.

14. The third USN aircraft carrier involved in Operations Attain Document I/II/III – and, indeed, in all major US military operations in the Mediterranean since October 1985 – USS *Saratoga*, ended her scheduled, six-month cruise and returned to the USA in early April 1986.

15. When considering possible deployments or re-deployments of USN aircraft carriers and their CVBGs, it should be kept in mind that the planning of Operations Attain Document I/II/III was heavily dependent on availability of aircraft carriers deployed with

the 6th Fleet in the Mediterranean. For example, it was only during Operation Attain Document III that three carriers became available and the USN felt strong enough to directly confront Libya. However, such a concentration of naval power was unusual and only became possible because the carrier battle group (CVBG) centred around USS *America* (CV-66) was rushed to join the CVBGs of USS *Coral Sea* (CV-43) and USS *Saratoga* (CV-60) in the Mediterranean several weeks early. Deployments of USN aircraft carriers are planned years in advance. They necessitate a huge deal of pre-planning for recruiting, training and deployment of thousands of aviators and seamen, acquisition and maintenance of hundreds of aircraft and helicopters, dozens of warships and preparation of immense amounts of supplies and spares. Changes in their schedules are thus extremely hard to achieve.

16. 'Weinberger, Crowe Provide Additional Details on Libya Raid', *Aerospace Daily*, 26 June 1986.
17. Although theoretically able to use AIM-9 Sidewinder and AIM-7 Sparrow air-to-air missiles, and capable of carrying a 20mm M61 Vulcan cannon in the weapons bay, for most of its career – and despite its 'fighter' designation – the F-111 was exclusively used as a bomber.
18. Dale Thompson, 'Operation Ghost Rider', usafaclasses.org. This and all subsequent quotations from Thompson are based on the same article.
19. Davis, p. 50.
20. Ibid, p. 47.
21. Ibid, p. 48.
22. While many Americans wondered how France denied the overflight permission, considering that the country found itself frequently hit by terrorist attacks, Richard Bernstein wrote in his article 'French Say they Favoured Stronger Attack on Libya' (*NYT*, 23 April 1986), that French President Francois Mitterrand actually 'opposed limited action', but showed readiness to support the US action if this would be 'aimed at a major change in Libya' – meaning the removal of Gaddafi from power.
23. While the serials of nearly all of the F-111Fs and EF-111As involved in the Libya raid are known, those of involved tanker aircraft appear never to have been released. The following serials were observed at RAF Fairford and Mildenhall between 10 and 17 April 1986: KC-135A: 00364, 10295, 10298, 38000, 38022, 38018, 38878, 38880, 38881, 38884, 63600, 63603, 63615, 63653, 71439, 71501, 72602, 80023, 80056, 80079, 91501; KC-135Q: 00342, 80050, 80094, 80117, 80125, 91513, 91520; KC-10A: 20191, 20193, 30075, 30076, 30077, 30078, 30079, 30080, 30082, 40186 (green top side), 40190, 40191, 50027, 50029, 50030, 50031, 60027, 90434, 91710, 91712, 91713, 91949, 91950.
24. Although numerous, and sometimes expressed by well-placed sources in France, reports that at least some of the involved aircraft used French airspace, or at least passed along the Franco-Spanish border in the Pyrenees, remain unconfirmed. If something of this kind happened, it must be one of the best-kept military secrets of the 1980s.
25. Stanik, p. 185.
26. 'Italy helped save Gaddafi by warning of US air raid', *Monsters and Critics*, 30 October 2008; 'Italy Warned Libya of Bombing, Saved Gaddafi's Life', *Bloomberg News*, 4 November 2008; 'Libya thanks Malta for warning of US bombing', *Times of Malta*, 21 January 2010.
27. 'Operation Prairie Fire', *VKO*, No. 4/17, 2004. As described in Part 1, the actual reason why neither the Soviets nor Libyans were able to provide a satisfactory solution for the critical deficiencies of the LAAF during clashes with the US Navy is that during the early 1980s the USA's Central Intelligence Agency (CIA) obtained an almost unbeatable source of the most sensitive intelligence about nearly all crucial Soviet air warfare weapons systems. The intelligence obtained in this fashion not only enabled the Americans to develop highly effective electronic countermeasures (ECM) against the most advanced Soviet weapons systems, but caused damage from which the military aviation sector of the USSR never recovered. Because all of their major combat aircraft and missiles were of Soviet origin, the conclusion is that the Libyans could not have fared any better even if they had been far better trained and prepared for fighting against the US military than they were.
28. Koldunov, 'Information', p. 1; although the Soviets delivered equipment for four battalions of V-200VE Vega long-range SAMs (ASCC-code SA-5 Gamon) in 1985, only one of these was operational by April 1986, positioned near the Ghurdabiyah AB outside Syrte. This site was much too far away from Tripoli and could only target aircraft flying at high altitudes south-west of Benghazi.
29. Originally, the USS *America* was to launch a total of seven A-6Es in this attack, but one aborted while still on the deck of the carrier due to a problem with its TRAM turret.
30. Stanik, p. 185.
31. Koldunov, 'Information', p. 1.
32. 'How I Bombed Qaddafi: A Personal Account of an American Blow Against Terrorism', *Popular Mechanics*, July 1987.
33. Davis, p. 56.
34. 'How I Bombed Qaddafi: A Personal Account of an American Blow Against Terrorism', *Popular Mechanics*, July 1987.
35. Ibid.
36. During the post-strike debrief, the pilot was asked why he flew at 660 knots over the USN warship positioned to 'de-louse' the

strikers exiting the Tripoli area from possible LAAF interceptors. His answer was, 'Because it wouldn't do 661 knots.' Davis, p. 58.

37. Roberto Suro, 'Attack on Libya: Changing a Future Course', *NYT*, 16 April 1986.

38. 'Waiting for the Retaliation', *Chicago Tribune*, 11 September 1986.

39. Stanik, p. 189.

40. Davis, p. 59.

41. 'How I Bombed Qaddafi: A Personal Account of an American Blow Against Terrorism', *Popular Mechanics*, July 1987; Laurel Wilson, 'Air Force Pilot helps unveil F-111, recalls 1986 Libya Raid', *The Daily News*, 15 June 2013.

42. Stanik, p. 190. Although Captain Lorence's fate remains unclear because his body was never recovered, an autopsy after the return of Captain Ribas-Dominici's body to the USA in 1989, via the Vatican, concluded that he had drowned in an unconscious state, without suffering any injuries that could be associated with their F-111F hitting the water surface at high speed. Furthermore, post-mission checks revealed that many of the ALQ-131s had failed – and indeed fell apart – due to the prolonged beating they had received from high-speed airflow during the mission; see Davis, p. 58.

43. Laurel Wilson, 'Air Force Pilot helps unveil F-111, recalls 1986 Libya Raid', *The Daily News*, 15 June 2013.

44. Davies, p. 60, Stanik, pp. 190-191

45. Roberto Suro, 'Attack on Libya: Changing a Future Course', *NYT*, 16 April 1986.

46. 'Operation Prairie Fire', *VKO*, No. 4/17, 2004.

47. Stanik, p. 192.

48. A G.222 and a F.27 transport each were destroyed at Benina AB.

49. 'Current Conflict Reprises 1986 US-Libya Clash', *AP*, 23 March 2011.

50. James O'Shea, 'Full Effect of Mission Unknown', *Chicago Tribune*, 16 April 1986.

51. Drendell, *Intruder*, p. 58.

52. Dee L. Mewbourne continued a successful career with the USN, later serving as commander of squadron VAQ-139 (during his tenure that squadron was awared the Battle E, Safety S, Golden Anchor and Prowler Tactical Excellence awards) and then as captain of USS *Eisenhower* (CVN-69).

53. Stanik, p. 193.

54. The leaking hot-air pipe was repaired later in the day, and the aircraft was then picked up by another crew for a flight back to Lakenheath.

55. Brian Shull, 'How a Pilot Risked His Life to Spy on Libya', Gizmodo.com, April 2010.

56. Ougartchinska et al., pp. 145-159; according to Ougartchinska, Gaddafi appreciated Ichpekov's expression of solidarity very much and thanked him in a 'special way': two months after the US strike, a Libyan Il-76 suddenly appeared above Sofia, the Bulgarian capital, and requested permission to land. Although friendly to him, the Bulgarians knew that Gaddafi was also unpredictable. Therefore, although granting landing permission, they put their police on alert and surrounded the aircraft – only to find it full of fresh oranges! Gaddafi's present was most welcome in Bulgaria, where imported oranges (usually from Cuba) were very expensive.

57. Unless otherwise stated, this chapter is based on cross-examination of information provided by the following sources of reference: Massimo Dini, 'Istruivo I Libici per conto di Roma', *Europeo*, 28 July 1990; Fabrizio Di Ernesto, *Portaerei Italia: Sessant'anni di NATO nel nostro Paese* (Milano: Fuoco Edizioni, 2011); Fulvio Martini, 'Sigonella 1985 – Cosi fermammo gli USA', *La Republica*, 16 April 2003; Riccardo Nicoli, *Cocardi Tricolori Speciale 2: F-104S* (Novara: RN Publishing, 2007); Riccardo Nicoli, *Cocardi Tricolori Speciale 4: F-104G* (Novara: RN Publishing, 2010); Cesario Piccinno & Paola Pentimela Testa, 'La strana storia dei pilot di Gheddafi', *Avvenimenti*, 27 July 1993; Daniele Protti & Sandro Provvisionato, 'Nemico, ti insegno a uccidere', *Europeo*, 21 July 1990; Franco Storaro, *1964–1984: Vent'anni di Aeronautica Militare – Missione Africa* (Roma: Instituto Bibliografico Napoleone, 2010); Domenico Valente & Pietro Pozzi, *Lockheed-Aeritalia, F-104 Starfighter* (Milano: Intergest, 1976). As well as for air and ground forces, the Italian Navy was mobilized too, and deployed warships that acted as radar pickets in the Sicily Strait, further protected through guided missile cruisers of the Andrea Doria-class and guided missile destroyers of the Audace-class. The Italian Rapid Intervention Force (the Forza d'Intervento Rapido, FIR) of 10,000 troops supported by CH-47, Agusta-Bell AB.205 and AB.212 helicopters, ran a major exercise on Sicily in July 1986, training for neutralization of a simulated Libyan commando attack infiltrated either by parachute or from the sea.

58. This air defence system became operational in summer 1986, and was initially under the command of General Giorgio Malorgio.

59. The only major unit of the Italian Army deployed on Sicily in early 1986 – the Aosta Motorized Brigade, equipped with old M47 tanks of US origin – was reinforced through deployment of the 6th Gruppo Squadroni with 42 Leopard I tanks. The Italian-Libyan crisis of 1986 later resulted in the Aosta Brigade also being re-equipped with Leopards.

60. Protti et all, 'Nemico, ti insegno a uccidere', Europeo Journal, 21 July 1990.

61. T. Cooper, 'Baghdad contre Téhéran: la guerre des villes', *Air Combat* No. 8/September–October 2014.

62. By 1987, the Chadian military had received four Panhard ERC-90s, 50 AML-90s, six AML-20s, eight Cadillac V-150 armoured

cars and an unknown number of 105mm M101 howitzers, 106mm recoilless guns and HOT anti-tank guided missiles (ATGMs). The FANT was always organized into battalions, and never operated larger formations. Even in 1987, there were only four of these 400-strong units, two of which were trained in Zaire. The bulk of the force was organized into some 127 companies, each about 150-strong. The 3,600-strong Presidential Guard operated its own armoured squadron equipped with a few Panhard M3 VTTs armed with 20mm cannons and HOT ATGMs (see *CIA World Factbook, 'Chad: a Country Study'*, Washington, 1988, pp. 178-202).

63. It is notable that the 1er RPIMa is a 'special forces'-type unit, similar to the Special Air Service (SAS) in Great Britain. At least officially, the team from the 1er RPIMa was deployed to Chad with the task of 'reconditioning' and providing 'operational assistance' to Chadian units equipped with FIM-92A Stinger MANPADs (or 'SATCP' in French military terminology). However, as far as is known, the FANT did not receive any Stingers before September 1987. Furthermore, it is possible that the team from the 54e RT was operationally supervised by the DGSE's 'Service Action' during deployment to Chad; see Mantoux, p. 85.

64. Jaguar As came to N'Djamena together with brand-new AS.30L guided missiles and Atlis II targeting pods in what was the first combat deployment for both of these.

65. Patrick du Morne Vert, *Mission Oxygène*, pp. 72-75.

66. A direct descendant of the 'Special Duties Flight' of the Free French from the Second World War, the GAM.56 is under operational command of the DGSE. As of 1986–1987, it flew aircraft and helicopters (hence 'mixed'), including C.160 Transalls, de Havilland Canada DHC-6 Twin Otters and SA.330 Pumas, and is known to have had pilots qualified to fly C-130 Hercules.

67. Ahmad Allam-Mi, *Tchad en Guerre*, pp. 315-321.

68. AdA Transalls are known to have delivered a load of eight Milan ATGM launchers and several 120mm mortars – together with related ammunition – during one of the flights in question. USAF transports flew in ammunition donated to Chad by Iraq, and stored in Cairo.

69. Ahmad Allam-Mi, *Tchad en Guerre*, pp. 322-325.

70. Ibid, pp. 332-333, Turner, pp. 175-176.

71. *Rubrique Historique de Guerrelec*, Bulletin Issue No. 11.

72. Goutx, interview, March 2014. It seems that the efforts of French pilots were even more frustrated by their superior commanders, who – irrespective of provocative Libyan operations south of the Red Line – repeatedly refused to issue orders for Mirages to intercept any of the many LAAF aircraft active north of the Red Line.

73. ADAM stood for Auto Directeur Amélioré (Improved Automatic Direction Finder).

74. Post-mission analysis concluded that it was probably Libyan military intelligence that warned Wadi Doum about an incoming strike after sighting the take-off of Jaguars from Bangui early in the morning. This was rather unusual because locally based AdA fighter-bombers were primarily active during the afternoons.

75. Carbon, interview, November 2013; this and all subsequent quotations from Carbon are based on transcriptions of the same interview.

76. The Jaguar strike on Tanoua AB was cancelled on direct order from Paris, which – attempting to measure its response to Libyan provocations and avoid an all-out war – offered the AdA the choice of striking either Tanoua or Wadi Doum, but not both of them.

77. It is notable that all available French sources identify this radar only by its ASCC-code, 'Flat Face' – without making a distinction between Flat Face-A (P-15) and Flat Face-B (P-19). As far as is known, the Libyans had at least one P-19 at Wadi Doum, while the presence of any P-15 there remains unconfirmed.

78. Former LAAF air defence officer, name withheld for reasons of personal safety. The officer in question observed the following: I read a few accounts of that attack published in the French press ever since, and [the] conclusion was clear: the French should have known that they had hit our Straight Flush, not the Flat Face. In one of [the] publications in question, French pilot Goutx was cited stating that the P-19 he fired at was 'working in impulse mode'. Well, the P-19 cannot switch to the continuous wave mode. The only radar in our service at Wadi Doum that could do so was the Straight Flush – and that was the radar knocked out during that attack. Another source observed that the missile actually failed to hit the antenna, but homed on the roof of the cab nearby, which reflected radar emissions. Finally, contrary to some commentaries subsequently published in the West, this attack did not 'blind Libyan air defences for months' (see M. Brecher & J. Wlikenfeld, *A Study in Crisis*, University of Michigan Press), nor 'prevented the LAAF from playing much role in the battle' (Pollack, p. 392). It was foremost a warning for the Libyans to cease bombing targets south of the Red Line.

79. According to a source that used to serve with 11e Choc in Chad at the time, no French troops or aircraft were deployed in this area or became involved in any of the above-mentioned shooting-downs of LAAF aircraft.

80. Ahmad Allam-Mi, *Tchad en Guerre*, pp. 332-333.

81. Ahmat M Yacoub Dabio, 'Libyan Prisoner Recalls the Fall of Wadi Doum', Dabio.net.

82. FANT, *Le Heros*, p. 4, and Patrick Mercillon, *Le Milan au Combat: la légende d'un missile* (Boulogne: ETAI Publishers, 1997), pp. 437; some contemporary Chadian releases have also cited the destruction of three MiG-23s at Wadi Doum, but such claims were never

confirmed. Overall, between 20 December 1986 and 30 March 1987, the FANT recorded 4,469 Libyans KIA and 936 captured, against 77 of their own losses and 132 wounded.

83. Dufour, interview, August 2014. A few days after liberating Faya Largeau, a FANT column patrolling desert tracks north of the oasis discovered an entire column of 12 T-55s and three 9K39 Strela-10 (ASCC-code SA-13) transport-erector launcher (TEL) vehicles – abandoned intact. The French immediately deployed one of their Military Assistance teams to the site, and Lieutenant Rouzeau – an officer specialized in the Crotale SAM-system – was put in charge of extracting all useful information out of it. The officer in charge of this operation, Lieutenant Colonel Dufor, recalled: At that time, it was unknown to us even that the Soviets had entrusted any SA-13s to Libyans. Because it took several months to complete our studies of this system, and it was necessary to protect Lieutenant Rouzeau during his work, time and again [we] deploy[ed] new teams from Kalait to Faya with [the] help of Transall transports.

84. Ahmad Allam-Mi, *Tchad en Guerre*, pp. 334-339.

85. Collectiv, *Le Jaguar dans ses Missions de Guerre Electronique* (Paris: Lavauzelle, 2007), pp. 195-198. Working without any of the necessary manuals, French technicians – supported by an Israeli team that provided lots of basic knowledge about Soviet SAMs in general – gradually managed to fully restore all equipment and make it fully operational. The site was tested against various French and Israeli ECM-systems and became a target for mock attacks of a Jaguar A flown by Lieutenant Colonel Serge Cocault, Deputy CO CEAM.

86. Although some of the losses in question were often credited to 'French Stinger teams' by various sources, the 11e Choc did not became involved in any of these shoot-downs. Notable losses in combat and the spate of defeats resulted in a series of defections from the LAAF in 1987. On 2 March, a crew of five flew their C-130H to Egypt, where two of them requested political asylum. On 29 March, three officers defected to Egypt flying a CH-47C Chinook helicopter. On 16 July 1987, three other officers followed on board a Mi-8 helicopter. Finally, on 1 March 1988, no less than four LAAF MiG-23MLs landed at Marsa Matruh AB in north-western Egypt. While Cairo initially claimed that all four pilots requested political asylum, Tripoli countered with explanations citing bad weather and lack of fuel. Eventually, the Libyans exchanged 36 Egyptian workers arrested on charges of espionage for most of these aircraft and all four MiG-23-pilots.

87. Related efforts led to ceasefire negotiations in Algiers, starting in 19 March 1987.

88. Despite a partial withdrawal of their troops from Chad, the AdA maintained the presence of eight Mirage F.1Cs at N'Djamena through most of 1987. Two of these were always held on quick-reaction alert (QRA), ready to take off within five minutes after alerted, and two others ready to take off within 15 minutes. Mirages were even more active by night: two fighters were held on a CAP north of N'Djamena every night between 1800 and 0600, while four were held on QRA +5.

89. Ahmad Allam-Mi, *Tchad en Guerre*, pp. 350-351 and pp. 365-371.

90. *Revue des anciens élèves de l'École l'Air*, No. 207 (December 2011). Interceptions of Libyan radio communications revealed that the crew of the Il-76 was scared by Mirages firing their cannons across the nose of their aircraft. They reported the presence of French interceptors and 'strongly recommended' all other Libyan aircraft to avoid the area. Several Chadian military leaders subsequently criticized French pilots for failing to destroy the big Ilyushin, some accusing them of 'collusion with the enemy'. Habré was very satisfied with precisely this kind of action, and – indeed – not a single Libyan aircraft approached Faya for days or even weeks afterwards.

91. Sené, p. 289.

92. The Mi-25 in question was claimed as shot down by FIM-43A Red Eye on 17 August 1987.

93. Ahmad Allam-Mi, *Tchad en Guerre*, pp. 350-351 and pp. 365-371. According to different reports, at least two Yugolsav and one East German citizens were captured during this raid and flown out to N'Djamena. The West German Ambassador to Chad expressly requested information about several West German engineers employed at the base, but it seems that all of them were killed.

94. Colonel Petit, 'Le succès du HAWK au TCHAD', *Supplément à Objectif Doctrine, Les cahiers du Retex No. 6* (Ministère de la Défense/ Armée de Terre, date of issue unknown); Colonel Petit & Lieutenant Colonel Dufour, 'L'Épervier et la Faucon', *Cesane Association/ Memorial Sol-Air* (http://cesane.artillerie.asso.fr). It is notable that the French had recovered the flight plan of the downed Tu-22. This had shown that the pilot was homing on the TACAN emitter of N'Djamena IAP. Furthermore, different French sources indicate that the Libyan pilot saw the incoming HAWK, began an evasive manoeuvre and deployed chaff and flares, but this was not enough. French reports have credited the LAAF crew as 'highly professional' and 'very courageous', while engaged in a 'very difficult, near suicidal mission'.

95. After the loss of one Tu-22 over N'Djamena on 7 September 1987, the LAAF never deployed any of its supersonic bombers in combat again. Seven surviving Tu-22s were stored at al-Jufra/Hun AB in early 1988. The last two were held on alert at Mitiga AB for a year longer until both were unceremoniously pushed aside and left to rot. The whereabouts of one example remain unknown, but it seems that the Tu-22 in question crashed inside Libya after running out of fuel, sometime in 1986.

96. Berry Schneider, *Weapons of Mass Destruction*.

97. Antoine, interviews, October & December 2013.

98. Ahmad Allam-Mi, *Tchad en Guerre*, pp. 372-402. As since discovered, the CIA subsequently convinced a large number of Libyan soldiers held as prisoners of war in Chad to defect. When Gaddafi demanded their return, they were flown out to Zaire (the Democratic Republic of Congo), where about half of them decided to return to Libya. Haftar and others then aligned themselves with the Libyan National Salvation Front, creating a force of about 2,000, based at a camp near Am Sinene (on the outskirts of N'Djamena), well equipped with the usual mix of Toyota 4WDs and automatic weaponry. However, when US financial aid to this group was stopped in the late 1980s, Haftar and about 300 of his soldiers had to escape to Kenya, from where they were permitted to emigrate to the USA in 1990. For details, see Mohammed Madi, 'Profile: Libya's renegade General Khalifa Haftar', *BBC News*, 20 May 2014.

99. Ali Thani, interview, July 2001. Thani continued his career with the LAAF until 1992, when he defected to Egypt, flying a stolen Cessna 172 (together with his wife and two sons). Ad-Dia spent two years as a POW in Chad before being given political asylum in France.

100. Ahmad Allam-Mi, *Tchad en Guerre*, pp. 372-380.

101. Ibid, pp. 381-395.

102. Identity of source withheld out of concerns for personal safety; interview, June 2013.

103. Creation of this force was strongly supported by Habré. The Chadian president grew ever more paranoid over time and suspected nearly everybody of plotting coups against him. He therefore deployed the FANT to carry out a brutal campaign of suppression against all dissident groups, but especially Chadian Christians. Furthermore, his Presidential Guard even carried out brutal crackdowns against several officials and leading FANT commanders. After dozens of villages were burned and thousands of civilians massacred in the Guera area, many survivors ended up in Libya, where they joined the Neo-GUNT.

104. Ahmad Allam-Mi, *Tchad en Guerre*, pp. 396-400.

105. Ibid, p. 401.

106. Ibid, p. 402.

107. James Ciment (ed), *World Terrorism: An Encyclopedia of Political Violence from Ancient Times to the Post-9/11 Era* (Oxon: Routledge, 2015), p. 348.

108. Clyde R. Mark, 'CRS Issue Brief for Congress: Libya', *Congressional Research Service & The Library of Congress*, 10 April 2002, p. 4.

109. Kenneth R Timmerman, 'The Poison Gas Connection: Western Suppliers of Unconventional Weapons and Technologies to Iraq and Libya', *Middle East Defence News*, 1990, & *Weapons of Mass Destruction: The Cases of Iran, Syria, and Libya* (Los Angeles: Simon Wiesenthal Center, 1992), p. 80.

110. 'Bleche, Nieten und Muttern', *Der Spiegel*, 16 January 1989. Ironically, the French government proved less inclined to follow the West German example. In December 1989, after accusing Paris of holding back delivery of two Mirage 5s and one Mirage F.1 since 1986, Libya imposed a ban on all French ships from its territorial waters. After negotiations, Paris gave up and not only permitted delivery of the three jets – in March 1990 – but subsequently granted permission for the Dassault company to respect its maintenance contracts with the LAAF, and even deploy a team of technical advisors to Libya. The team in question remained in the country until at least 1996, helping Libyan technicians to perform depot-level work on their Mirages. The work of Dassault's team was one of the major reasons why the LAAF continued operating its Mirage 5s and F.1s, even after it was forced to store most of its MiG-21s, MiG-23s and MiG-25s, in the mid-1990s. Nevertheless, French publications indicate that the utilization of the remaining Mirages remained low, while their attrition was very high: no less than 31 Mirage 5s (including 21 Mirage 5Ds and three Mirage 5DEs) were written off in different accidents and combat between 1970 and 2003. By mid-2003, only 16 Mirage 5s were still operational – all concentrated with the Mitiga-based No. 1001 Squadron. Libya was then approached by Pakistan with an offer to buy the surviving aircraft. Following short negotiations, the Pakistanis purchased 53 Mirage in June 2004 and 26 later the same year, together with extensive stocks of spares (including about 50 de-facto brand-new, never before used engines). By that time, the LAAF fleet had flown a total of only about 72,000 hours – or about 600 hours per average airframe. For these and other details, see Chenel et al., *Mirage III/5/50*, pp. 206-210.

111. Enright, interview, September 2006; most of the following reconstruction is based on the same interview, provided during the Tomcat Sunset Symposium at NAS Oceana.

112. It remains unknown whether the Libyans launched a SAR operation for their two downed MiG-23MF-pilots. The usual version of the USN indicates that both of them drowned, but there are rumours that one was eventually recovered by Libyan helicopters.

113. According to reports from Sudanese sources, at least 12 MiG-23MSs and several MiG-25s were evacuated all the way to Sudan. While the MiG-23s were subsequently donated to the Sudanese Air Force, the MiG-25s – after flying some reconnaissance sorties over the south of that country – were returned to Libya in 1991.

AUTHORS

Tom Cooper

Tom Cooper, from Austria, is a military-aviation analyst and historian. Following a career in worldwide transportation business – in which, during his extensive travels in Europe and the Middle East, he established excellent contacts – he moved into writing. An earlier fascination with post-Second World War military aviation has narrowed to focus on smaller air forces and conflicts, about which he has collected extensive archives of material. Concentrating primarily on air warfare that has previously received scant attention, he specialises in investigative research on little-known African and Arab air forces, as wella s the Iranian air force. Cooper has published 23 books – including the unique 'Arab MiGs' series, which examined the development and service history of major Arab air forces in conflicts with Israel – as well as over 250 articles on related topics, providing a window into a number of previously unexamined yet fascinating conflicts and relevant developments.

Albert Grandolini

Military historian and aviation-journalist, Albert Grandolini, was born in Vietnam and gained an MA in history from Paris I Sorbonne University. His primary research focus is on contemporary conflicts in general and particularly on the military history of Asia. Having spent his childhood in South Vietnam, the Vietnam War has been one of his main fields of research. He is the author of the books Fall of the Flying Dragon: South Vietnamese Air Force (1973–1975) with Harpia Publishing and the two volumes on Vietnam's Easter Offensive of 1972 with Helion Publishers in the Asia@War Series, and is also co-author of the three volumes of the Libyan Air Wars with Helion Publishers in the Africa@War Series. He has also written numerous articles for various British, French and German magazines, such as Air Enthusiast, Flieger Revue Extra, Fana de l'aviation, Tank Zone and Batailles et Blindés. He has regularly contributed to the Air Combat Information Group (ACIG) and the Au Delà de la Colline military history French website.

Arnaud Delalande

Arnaud Delalande is researcher and author from Tours in France. Military history, and the history of military aviation in particular have long been his passion, especially airpower in Africa and in former French colonies. Except for working as editor of 'Aéro Histo' blog (http://aerohisto.blogspot.fr) and contributor of 'Alliance Geostrategique' blog (alliancegeostrategique.org) in his spare time, he has become one of few foreigners with deeper interest in the history of recent Chadian wars, as well as French military operations in that country. He has published several related articles in specialized French magazines such as Air Fan, and Air Combat. He is also co-author of the three volumes of the Libyan Air Wars with Helion Publishers in the Africa@War Series.